NICK ENRIGHT (1950–2003) trained for the theatre at New York University School of Arts after early experience in Australia including with Nimrod and Melbourne Theatre Company. He was an actor, director and teacher as well as a writer. His plays include *On the Wallaby, Daylight Saving, St James Infirmary, Mongrels, A Property of the Clan, The Quartet from Rigoletto, Blackrock, Good Works, Spurboard* and *A Man with Five Children*. With Justin Monjo he adapted Tim Winton's *Cloudstreet* for the stage. He also wrote for film and television, including co-writing with George Miller the screenplay for *Lorenzo's Oil* which was nominated for an Oscar. He wrote a number of musicals including *The Venetian Twins* and *Summer Rain* with composer Terence Clarke. He wrote the book for the Australian production of *The Boy from Oz*.

Among many awards were two Green Room Awards for Best Play, four Gold AWGIE Awards, the 1998 Sidney Myer Performing Arts Award and the NSW Premier's Special Award.

As well as being a prolific writer, Nick Enright was a noted acting teacher, particularly at NIDA and WAAPA.

Greg Stone as Shane Grogan and Paul English (foreground) as Tim Donovan in the 1995 Playbox Theatre Company production at the CUB Malthouse, Southbank, Melbourne. (Photo: Jeff Busby)

GOOD WORKS
NICK ENRIGHT

Currency Press, Sydney

CURRENCY PLAYS

First published in 1995
by Currency Press Pty Ltd,
PO Box 2287, Strawberry Hills, NSW, 2012, Australia
enquiries@currency.com.au
www.currency.com.au

in association with Playbox Theatre Centre, Melbourne.

This edition first published in 2015

Cataloguing-in-publication data for this title is available from the National Library of Australia website: www.nla.gov.au.

Typeset by Dean Nottle for Currency Press.
Cover design by Studio Emma.
Cover image of boy by Helen White Photography for Darlinghurst Theatre Company.
Cover image of man from iStock, copyright: duncan1890.

Every reasonable effort has been made to ensure that permission has been obtained where possible for production photos in this publication. If you believe that your rights have been infringed, please contact Currency Press at the address above.

Currency Press acknowledges the Traditional Owners of the Country on which we live and work. We pay our respects to all Aboriginal and Torres Strait Islander Elders, past and present.

Contents

Stephen Jackson (standing) as Tim Donovan, Colin Moody (seated on bike) as Shane Grogan, and Ingrid Mason as Mary Margaret in the 1995 Queensland Theatre Company production at the Cremorne Theatre, South Brisbane. (Photo: Reina Irmer, reproduced by permission of Queensland Theatre Company)

INTRODUCTION

Anne Pender

Good Works

Nick Enright's *Good Works* is a savage play about families and friendships. It considers questions of loyalty, betrayal and the real meaning of goodness. The action of the play explores the relationship between two young men, Tim and Shane, and the friendship between their mothers, Mary Margaret and Rita.

Good Works is compelling in its exploration of sexuality in both generations and the pressure to conform imposed by authority figures on all of the characters. Its rapidly paced shifts in time and place create dramatic tension, a dynamic energy in the play and an ingenious sharpness of focus on the moral questions that infuse the drama.

The play was first produced in 1994 and is important in the history of Australian theatre in that its focus is on two young homosexual men. One of its early scenes takes place in a gay pub where the two main protagonists meet up unexpectedly after many years. Although Tim is certain that the man is his old school friend, Shane refuses to admit to his identity to Tim in the pub, instead posing as someone called 'John' as the two of them engage in a ritual of charged sexual banter.

> TIM: … you're a good-looking man. That's not a line, it's a
>   compliment. What if it was a line? Are you available?
> SHANE: You don't waste time.
> TIM: No-one does in this joint. So, are you?
> SHANE: Am I what? Queer?
> TIM: That's a bit conceptual for me. Let's start with available.
> SHANE: Could be. Some nights I'm… you know, not sure
>   what I'm after. (p.4)

The action of the play spans more than fifty years and three generations in the lives of two Catholic families: the Donovans and the Kennedys. It carefully juxtaposes the friendship between the two young women and the boys who are their sons. Mary Margaret (mother of Tim) is an orphan brought up by nuns. She is obedient and well-behaved. Her best friend Rita (mother of Shane) is more daring and headstrong, and flouts the strictures of appropriate behaviour for a young woman in a country town during the years before the War. Later Rita returns to her home town to bring up her son Shane on her own. By this time Mary Margaret has married Neil Donovan, a successful man; they try to convince Rita to let Shane live with them in a more 'stable' environment, given that Shane has been the victim of an angry attack by Rita's boyfriend.

The critical revelation in the play comes towards the end of the drama when Shane discovers Tim being beaten by one of their teachers, Brother Clement. When Shane attempts to intervene to protect his friend the teacher knocks him to the ground where he cuts his head on broken glass. Furious, Shane stabs Brother Clement and fatally wounds him. Shane is convicted of murder and sent to gaol. It emerges that no-one stands up for Shane in court and all the relationships are shattered.

Throughout the two acts of the play the bonds between the women and the young men are portrayed with a depth and clarity that make the various acts of betrayal all the more stark and tragic. Mary Margaret confesses her youthful love and admiration for Rita after the killing of her son's teacher by Shane: 'You told me I was lovely, but you, you were the loveliest thing I'd ever seen. You were a goddess' (p.58). Her anguish is poignant as she reveals her isolation and sense of smallness in the world: 'I'm not loved. You think I haven't always known that?' (p.59) She confesses her knowledge of the relationship between Rita and Neil when all of them were young, and the intensity of her love for Rita. She recalls hearing Neil coming home late at night after being with Rita: 'I'd lie there and hold myself, touch myself, seeing myself burning in the pits of Hell, but touching myself, wondering, what happened? What did he do to you?...' (p.59)

The incipient violence under the surface of the relationships between the men in the play explodes in the last scenes when Shane stabs their teacher using the knife his father has passed on to him, and later when he holds it to Tim's throat in the pub and calls him to account for his failure as a friend: 'Your whole fucken life, show me this, tell me why, hold me up, cut me loose, turn me on. And tonight take me home, let me in, just 'cause you think you know who I am' (p.61). In contrast the gentle snow that enchants the young boy Tim in the snow dome given to him by his grandmother offers a motif for the play and the swirling memories of its characters, each one imprisoned in his or her solitary misery. Theatre critic John McCallum describes the snow dome as the central metaphor of the play, reflecting the memories that 'are stirred … when you shake them up, but then settle when you let it rest' (McCallum 2009: 252). The motif of the snow dome also captures the way in which most of the characters are stuck in time, their good works so often symbolic rather than real, their sense of morality both fixed and fragile.

Enright questions the tyranny and cruelty of normative expressions of masculinity that keep individuals under control throughout the play, from Alan's admonishment in the gay pub to his friend not to speak openly about his childhood feelings: 'No personal slush. We're only interested in the collective memory…' (p.1), to Shane's physical abuse by his mother's boyfriend, to Tim's father's order to Brother Clement to chastise his son and eliminate any sign of the effeminate: '"Bring him down to earth, Brother. Make him one of us, Brother, that's your job"' (p.48), leading to his beating. The oppressiveness of social expectations on the women in their relationships with their partners and their sons is no less crippling, and sets the women in competition with one another for the attention and approval of the men.

In an interview Enright told Stephen Fenelly that *Good Works* was autobiographical. He said: 'I think [it is] probably commonly assumed by people who know me that I am represented on the stage by the rather timid, middle-class, repressed, gay, would-be artist, and sure that's an aspect of me, but the violent, vengeful, passionate kid with the knife is also me. And likewise the two women. They are equally representative of certain aspects of me, and I have to love and accept those bits of me in order to be able to put them on the stage' (quoted by Kiernander 2008: 121). The play explores the way in which people in real life perform roles and wear masks, a human phenomenon that intrigued Nick Enright. In fact this duality of human experience was something Enright struggled with in his own life. As Adrian Kiernander observes in an essay on Enright, it was in the theatre that the playwright creatively resolved the tension between the external show a person makes of him or herself and their inner being (Kiernander 2008: 123).

Nick Enright

Nick Enright's passion for drama began at the age of six when a neighbour visited his house with a simple home-made theatre constructed of a box with two rods in it. The neighbour was John Bell. It was Bell who inspired Enright to pursue work in the theatre when he completed his university degree and to join the Nimrod Theatre in Sydney.

Enright was born in Maitland, New South Wales on 22 December 1950, one of five children. As a teenager he was sent to board at St Ignatius College Riverview in Sydney where he excelled as a student. In the U.S. as a young man he studied with the playwright Israel Horovitz and, with his encouragement, began writing plays of his own. Enright also immersed himself in Strasberg's approach to acting using the Method and believed that an actor could 'bring life to the human soul—in circumstances created by the playwright' (Kingston 2005: 4). Within his own career Enright constantly moved between roles, from actor to director to writer to teacher and then back to director again. He is remembered as a man of exceptional talent who always gave total commitment and was unafraid of experimentation.

Enright strongly believed in the power of collaboration and stressed the creative strength of actors and directors in the community. He insisted on working with actors on his plays at the end of the writing process, involving them in the essential final stages of script development. He also believed in the 'aesthetic and political necessity' of producing Australian plays (interview with Kiernander 1992). Although he died young, at the age of fifty-two, Enright wrote ten plays, eleven musicals and seven scripts for television and film. He is one of the most successful, significant and versatile Australian playwrights.

Enright's interest in understanding his own life and personality inspired him to undertake six years of psychoanalysis. He believed that we are all 'prisoners… creatures of our own preoccupations and obsessions' (Kelly 1994: 63), a theme that is dominant in *Good Works*. His own enduring preoccupations were 'family and the fate of the young' (Kelly 1994: 63). Enright experienced depression at various stages of his life and expressed frustration at how this circumscribed the work of which he felt he was capable (Pender interview with Ian Enright 2005). In *A Man with Five Children*, one of his last plays,

Enright explores his ideas about family and fate. *Good Works* is also a study of personality, family and fortune. His musical *Variations,* first performed in 1982, considers women's roles in families in the context of the immense social change that had taken place over the two preceding decades. In spite of the changes in attitudes to women and increasing equality of opportunity for women in Australia in this period, Enright was forthright in his views about Australian men and what he perceived as a culture of destructive 'dislike' towards women. He observed that the 'real emotional energy' of men in Australian culture is towards other men (quoted in the *Courier Mail* 11 Apr 1997: 19). Many of his plays, including *Good Works,* portray this emotional energy amongst men with, in this play, another layer of homosexual energy complicating notions of hegemonic masculinity.

The play in performance

Good Works offers a number of challenges and innovations in its presentation of time, place and character. For example in spite of the large time span of the play, the actors must transform—within one line in some instances—to become older or younger according to the rapid shifts in time. Each jump highlights a fracture in a relationship or an important dramatic point. For example, in the 1981 pub scene at the beginning of the play Tim says to Shane (or 'John'): 'What's your mother's name?' Shane replies: 'What makes you think I had a mother?'

> *He tosses the snow dome in the air.* TIM *catches it.*
> *1962.* MRS KENNEDY *sees* RITA *and* SHANE *approaching her front gate.* (p.5)

Shane and his mother Rita appear back at her mother's house and the actor must instantly become a version of the character some nineteen years younger. He is now eleven.

Another challenge for actors is the doubling of roles. For example, in the first production of the play in 1994 the one actor, David Field, played Shane and Neil, Tim's father. Similarly Jamie Jackson played the characters Tim and Eddie, Shane's father. This doubling further complicates the fault lines between the two characters and the two generations, and makes the acting especially challenging.

The play contains strong dramatic speeches for individuals and for two characters, delivered in unison or chorally, such as when Mary

Margaret is reading out a letter from Neil to Rita. The stage direction
dictates that the *'actors and director should decide who says what'*.

> MARY MARGARET [*reading*] & NEIL: [*to* RITA, *shared*
> *dialogue*] 'Keep your body a mystery.' Isn't that what
> Mother John used to tell you girls? It's no mystery to me.
> I've got it all mapped out. Every night I explore it. I'd make
> a good explorer, Rita. And I know where I'd plant the flag.
> I see you walking away from me, rolling those hips. I see
> those other blokes staring at you, tongues hanging out,
> ready for a good long drink. It's bloody hard, Rita. And the
> longer I'm away, the harder it is. See?
>
> > MARY MARGARET *turns to a new page, stares at the*
> > *drawing.* NEIL *goes, his eye on Rita.* MARY MARGARET
> > *puts the letter away hastily.* (p.38)

The sensuality, amusing double entendre and longing in Neil's letter,
read out by Mary Margaret but possibly also spoken by Neil, captures
the sexual energy of the young people separated by the war service of
the men and Mary Margaret's envious shadowing of her friend as she
reads the letter to Rita.

The symbolic qualities of three props in the play allow for effective
and simple staging: the simple peg doll made by Rita for her friend
Margaret and presented to her in the opening scene when the two
characters are small girls is enigmatic and poignant, the tantalising
snow dome produced from Tim's pocket early on in the gay pub scene
has an attendant symbolic power, and the knife, passed from father to
son and used in an act of vengeful fury by a young man on his teacher
and again to threaten his old friend in a dramatic climax, is a powerful
symbol of male violence.

In production the dancing Dutch 'girls', the riverbank scenes and
the snow that falls at the end of the play offer many possibilities for
staging, scenography and projection. The symbolic power of snow
at Christmas and the nativity figures in this play also offer important
visual and thematic opportunities. They set in relief the struggles of the
characters to do good in their lives in the face of cruelty and crippling
memories, the oppressiveness of 'good behaviour' and their inability
to protect the vulnerable.

Good Works is perhaps Nick Enright's most powerful play. Its moral seriousness, tight narrative and rapid scene progression, its strong, memorable characters and its exploration of human vulnerability through vivid social realism offer an enduring challenge to performers and audiences.

Sydney
September 2015

Anne Pender is Associate Professor of English and Theatre Studies at the University of New England in Armidale, New South Wales.

Works Cited

Kelly, Veronica. 1994. 'A Form of Music: An Interview with Nick Enright', *Australasian Drama Studies* (April): 58:76.

Kiernander, Adrian. 'Enright on Record: Evidence from the Television Archives of the Australian Broadcasting Corporation' in Anne Pender and Susan Lever (eds.) *Nick Enright: An Actor's Playwright*, Amsterdam: Rodopi, 2008, pp. 115-126.

Kiernander, Adrian. 1992. Unpublished Interview with Nick Enright (17 November).

Kingston, Peter. 2005. 'Directing Nick Enright', *Dialogue* 64 (December), pp. 3-4.

McCallum, John. 2009. *Belonging: Australian Playwriting in the Twentieth Century*, Sydney: Currency Press.

Pender, Anne. 2005. Unpublished Interview with Ian Enright.

Further Reading

O'Sullivan, Jane. 2008. 'Mongrels and Young Curs: The Hounding of the Feminine in *St James Infirmary*, *Good Works*, *Blackrock* and *Spurboard*', in Anne Pender and Susan Lever (eds.), *Nick Enright: An Actor's Playwright*, Amsterdam: Rodopi, pp. 127-142.

Parr, Bruce. 1998. 'From Gay and Lesbian to Queer Theatre' in Veronica Kelly (ed.) *Our Australian Theatre in the 1990s*, Amsterdam: Rodopi, pp. 89-103.

Pender, Anne and Lever, Susan (eds.). 2008. *Nick Enright: An Actor's Playwright*, Amsterdam: Rodopi.

For Douglas Hedge, with thanks and love.

Good Works was first produced by the Q Theatre, Penrith, on 29 July 1994, with the following cast:

MARY MARGARET	Vanessa Downing
RITA	Kelly Butler
MOTHER JOHN / MRS KENNEDY / MRS DONOVAN	Maggie Dence
SHANE / NEIL	David Field
TIM / EDDIE	Jamie Jackson
ALAN / BROTHER CLEMENT / BARRY / MR DONOVAN	Danny Adcock

Director, Adam Cook
Designer, Genevieve Blanchett
Lighting Designer, Andrew Kinch
Music, Ian McDonald

CHARACTERS

MARY MARGARET

RITA KENNEDY

MRS KENNEDY, her mother

NEIL DONOVAN

MRS DONOVAN, his mother

MR DONOVAN, his father

MOTHER JOHN

BROTHER CLEMENT, a Marist brother

TIM DONOVAN, son to Mary Margaret and Neil

SHANE GROGAN, son to Rita

EDDE GROGAN, his father

ALAN

BARRY CARMODY

RECEPTIONIST, voice

SETTING

The play takes place in a large country town and a major city anywhere in Australia between 1928 and 1981.

ACT ONE

1928. RITA *approaches* MARY MARGARET, *holding out a peg doll.*

MARY MARGARET: It's a dolly.

RITA: Yes.

MARY MARGARET: With plaits.

RITA: I made those.

MARY MARGARET: Funny hat.

RITA: She's Dutch.

MARY MARGARET: What's her name?

RITA: She's for you. You give her a name.

> *She hands the doll to* MARY MARGARET *and runs away.*

MARY MARGARET: What will I call her?

> *1981. A gay pub.*

TIM: 'See, Mr Gitts, most people never have to face the fact that at the right time, the right place, they're capable of anything.' You need a clue? His name is really Gittes. Give in? Come on. Give in.

ALAN: I hate giving in.

TIM: I've heard different. John Huston in *Chinatown*.

ALAN: Unfair. Too recent.

TIM: Tough. Four-three.

> *From his pocket he brings a little snow dome which holds a nativity scene.*

I died holding this. Who am I? What did I say?

ALAN: 'Rosebud.' What is this, kindergarten?

TIM: I'm rebuilding your shattered confidence.

ALAN: Four-all. Do we allow props?

TIM: I didn't plan this. I picked it up on the way here. One of those trash-and-treasure places.

ALAN: Déjà Vu. Objets Trouvés…

TIM: It's a childhood thing. It reminded me of—

ALAN: No personal slush. We're only interested in the collective memory. This is a nativity scene. In *Kane* it's just an old log cabin. I'll take an extra point for that. Five-four. The theme from *Tammy*.

TIM *starts to whistle.*

Not whistled, sung, both choruses. I'm waiting.

He plays with the snow dome.

1962. TIM *plays the piano: the theme from* Tammy.

MARY MARGARET: Is that one of your practice pieces, Timothy?
TIM: No.
MARY MARGARET: Then why are you playing it?
TIM: Because.

TIM *sings a line or two from the song 'Tammy'.*

MARY MARGARET: Sometimes I wonder where you come from.
TIM: Uckpucka.
MARY MARGARET: What?
TIM: That's where I come from. Skittaswa. Grang grang grang.
MARY MARGARET: What?
TIM: It has its own language.
MARY MARGARET: What language?
TIM: Where I come from.
MARY MARGARET: Play your practice pieces.
TIM: Uckpucka skittaswa. Grang grang grang. Buddika pipalani.
MARY MARGARET: And stop that awful language.
TIM: You don't even know what I'm saying.

1981. Bar.

ALAN: [*as Bette Davis*] 'I was hiding behind screens before you were born.'
TIM: Bette.
ALAN: Brilliant. In what?
TIM: Something.
ALAN: Something. Shall I ask the room? There'd be twenty answers straight off. 'I was hiding behind screens before you were born.'
TIM: You got me.
ALAN: *Old Acquaintance.* Seven-four.
TIM: I like it. I'll use it. 'I was hiding behind screens before you were born.'
ALAN: Keep the gestures small, Tim-Tam. You're being checked out. A new face. Just your type.

TIM: I wasn't aware I had a type.

ALAN: You do. Trust mother. That's him. He's just west of Wally. Twenty-four. Builder's labourer. A few tatts where you'd expect to find them, a few where you wouldn't. First night on the street, yearning for just the right meld of tenderness and raunch.

TIM: Twenty-seven, bus driver, having a night off from the wife, wondering why every time he's at the dentist he picks up *Cleo* and turns straight to the centrefold.

ALAN: He's going. No, he's coming! Thirty. Between jobs. Good nick. Played a bit of sport, maybe boxing…

TIM: I know him. From somewhere.

ALAN: Some beat.

> SHANE *reaches them.*

He says he knows you. I'm Alan. This is Tim. And you're…? Hard work.

SHANE: John.

ALAN: He doesn't look like a John.

TIM: What does a John look like?

ALAN: John wears a suit, lives at home, works in an office, brings a cut lunch.

TIM: [*to* SHANE] That's not you. [*To* ALAN] I think someone wants you.

ALAN: So what do you do, John?

TIM: Someone's calling you.

ALAN: Only La Wally.

> TIM *glares at him.*

Oh. I think I'm what the French would call 'de tropp'.

> ALAN *goes.*

TIM: Sure we haven't met?

> SHANE *shakes his head.*

Why did you come across?

SHANE: Might have been heading out.

TIM: You were staring at me.

SHANE: You were staring at me.

TIM: Only because you were staring at me.

SHANE: Only because—

TIM: Someone stared first, we'll settle for that. Perhaps it was me. Well, you're a good-looking man. That's not a line, it's a compliment. What if it was a line? Are you available?

SHANE: You don't waste time.

TIM: No-one does in this joint. So, are you?

SHANE: Am I what? Queer?

TIM: That's a bit conceptual for me. Let's start with available.

SHANE: Could be. Some nights I'm… you know, not sure what I'm after.

TIM: At thirty?

SHANE: Thirty? You reckon?

TIM: I'm sure. Same age as me. I think I know you. Do I?

SHANE: Would you like to?

TIM *puts his hand to* SHANE*'s hairline.*

What the fuck… [are you doing?]

TIM: I thought I saw a scar.

SHANE: I got scars other places. You want to see them?

TIM: Maybe.

SHANE: Maybe you will, then. So what's your story?

TIM: Alan was right. You're not a John. You could be… someone else.

SHANE: We'll work something out. What do you do for a crust?

TIM: Shane. You could be Shane.

SHANE: Shane? No, mate. I been a lot of things. Not Shane. Not that I remember, anyway.

TIM: Sorry. Sorry, mate. Trick of the light.

SHANE: Who was he?

TIM: Someone I knew.

SHANE: Yeah…

TIM: A friend. No. More like a…

SHANE: What? Say it.

TIM: I don't know. We were like brothers. Whatever that means.

SHANE: You going to buy me a drink, or what?

TIM: I better be off…

SHANE: Home? On your own? No way.

TIM: Alan and Wally are over there. Seem to be calling me. I better go, John.

SHANE: You're not scared of me, Timmy? You weren't when you stared at me. Come across, that was the message. I come across and you back off.

TIM: Timmy.

SHANE: Eh?

TIM: You said Timmy.

SHANE: Your mate introduced you.

TIM: As Tim.

> SHANE *shrugs, plays with the snow dome.*

SHANE: Do you do coke?

TIM: 'Neiges d'Antan'. [*or: 'Snows of Yesteryear'*]

SHANE: Eh?

TIM: The shop where I bought this tonight. I just remembered.

SHANE: Do you do coke?

TIM: Coke rots your teeth. What's your mother's name?

SHANE: What makes you think I had a mother?

> *He tosses the snow dome in the air.* TIM *catches it.*

> *1962.* MRS KENNEDY *sees* RITA *and* SHANE *approaching her front gate.*

MRS KENNEDY: That car sounds crook.

RITA: It got us here. You look well. Extra well. Aren't you going to say hello to Shane? It's been a long time.

MRS KENNEDY: Hello, son.

RITA: He's thirsty, Mum. We've been driving all night.

MRS KENNEDY: I'll get him a glass of water.

> *She goes.*

RITA: She's taken the swing down. That won't matter to you, you're too old for swings. You tired? Sit down there. You'll have a bed soon.

> MRS KENNEDY *brings a glass of water.*

MRS KENNEDY: I'm on my way to Mass.

RITA: Weren't you expecting us?

MRS KENNEDY: I'm making the nine First Fridays. This is my ninth.

RITA: I wrote you a letter.

MRS KENNEDY: Did you now?

RITA: Barry Carmody's offered me a job. I wrote and asked you if we could stay here. Till we get sorted out.

MRS KENNEDY: Why can't the Carmodys put you up? They've got the room.

RITA: Barry offered us a caravan down the back of his yard. That might be a bit cramped, but. You know me, all arms and legs.

MRS KENNEDY *turns to* SHANE, *taking the glass.*

MRS KENNEDY: Wait in the car. Go on, son.

He goes.

I like your hide. Bringing the boy to the door.

RITA: I thought you'd be glad to see him at least.

MRS KENNEDY: Couldn't you have found a job somewhere else?

RITA: If you want a barney, wait till I've got a clear head.

MRS KENNEDY: Have you been drinking?

RITA: I've been driving. On an empty stomach. I'm skint. I had to borrow petrol money. Let us in, Mum. Just for a few hours.

MRS KENNEDY: I don't want to be late for Mass. And I don't want to turn up in a state. I'm not a hard woman, Rita. But you've caused me enough shame for one lifetime.

RITA: If you'd read what I wrote! This is a new leaf. A new job. A new start. I'm going to get this kid settled.

MRS KENNEDY: I'm pleased to hear it, Rita. But I've got no money to spare…

RITA: I'm not asking for money.

MRS KENNEDY: And I've got no room for you or him.

RITA: You loved him when he was little.

MRS KENNEDY: And you took him away from me.

RITA: This time'll be different.

MRS KENNEDY: I'm sure. This time I'll be responsible for a trail of debts up and down the coast, from—

RITA: You did get my letter.

MRS KENNEDY: I'm not going to be late. I'll remember you in my intentions. You've got no right to be here. Why are you here?

1962. The classroom. BROTHER CLEMENT. TIM *sits alone.* SHANE *appears.*

CLEMENT: This is our new boy. Shane Grogan. I see several vacant desks. One beside Fennelly… And there's Donovan, making a space for you, Grogan. Donovan wants to make a friend.

TIM *coughs.*

Donovan has a weak chest. Donovan's a martyr to bronchitis. But he's very musical, isn't that right, Donovan? [*Beat.*] Yes, Brother.

TIM: Yes, Brother.

CLEMENT: Donovan learns the piano at the convent. And he sang a song at the Coalfields Eisteddfod last year. Highly commended he was, covered himself with glory. What did you sing? Something sacred? Something Irish? What?

TIM: 'Tammy', Brother.

CLEMENT: 'Tammy'. Something off the films. Grogan, I'd sit there, next to Fennelly. He doesn't have Donovan's music, but he doesn't have all that phlegm on board either. Parse this sentence, boys. The farmer…

SHANE *sits next to* TIM.

SHANE: You hate him, don't you?

TIM *puts a finger to his lips.*

You hate his guts. But you're scared of him. Shit-scared. I can smell it on you. Now look at him. He's going to smell worse. There's a cocky sitting on his head.

TIM: What?

SHANE: He's got a cocky sitting on his head. Imagine. A dirty great cockatoo, sticking its chest out…

TIM: Shhh.

SHANE: … and its arse up… and pooping down his neck. A big, steamy, green-and-yellow nasty. Kiiiierk splat.

TIM *hoots.*

CLEMENT: The farmer was taking his cow to market because he hoped to sell it. Not much humour in that. The Strop certainly doesn't find it funny. But some boy found it funny. Who? A high musical laugh, Donovan. The Strop would like you to come up and explain the joke.

TIM *rises slowly.*

SHANE: Sit down.

He rises. TIM *stays standing.*

It was me.

CLEMENT: It was me, Brother.

Silence.

You're sure, Grogan?

SHANE: It was me, yeah.

CLEMENT: Come up and shake hands with The Strop.

> TIM *sees* SHANE *approach the desk. He follows, putting out his hand beside* SHANE*'s.*

Partners in crime? Very well. Partners in punishment.

> *1981.* TIM *and* SHANE *at the bar.*

SHANE: Listen, you've got beautiful eyes.

TIM: Thank you.

SHANE: So now you can stop staring, and buy me that drink.

TIM: Beer?

SHANE: Double scotch. Straight up. And then…

> *1962. They are outside the caravan.*

I'll show you this thing.

TIM: What is it?

SHANE: I told you. A thing.

TIM: What sort of a thing?

SHANE: You'll see. Once Mum's gone to work.

TIM: You live here? In a caravan. How many of you?

SHANE: Two. Me and my mum.

TIM: I've never been inside a caravan.

SHANE: Now's your chance.

TIM: I can't stay long. I'll be late.

> RITA *emerges with compact and purse.*

RITA: You and me both. I say let them wait.

> *She looks into her mirror.*

The light's crook in there. I look like Coco the Clown.

> *She sits to repair her make-up.*

Introduce your friend, Shane.

SHANE: I've forgotten his name. No. It's Timmy.

RITA: Hello, Timmy.

SHANE: Any Coke inside?

TIM: Coca-Cola rots your teeth.

RITA: But do you like it?

> *He nods.*

Then help yourself. I'm off. Have I got too much lippy on?
SHANE: Yes. You always do.

He goes inside the caravan.

TIM: I think you look beautiful.
RITA: Beautiful. Thank you.
TIM: Like a film star. What do you do, Mrs Grogan?
RITA: Three guesses. No, maybe not. I'm a barmaid at the Imperial. And
    I'm on at five so I'd better—
TIM: Five o'clock? Oh, God.
RITA: What? What, love?
TIM: I thought it was about four. We went to the quarry. I'm in real strife.
RITA: That sounds drastic.
TIM: I've missed my piano lesson.

SHANE emerges with Coke.

RITA: Have a drink and think of a good fib.

SHANE passes the bottle.

TIM: Oh, God. Hide this.

He gives the Coke to SHANE. MARY MARGARET *approaches.*

SHANE: Hide it?
RITA: What did you say your last name was?
TIM: I didn't see the time.
MARY MARGARET: You have a watch. Thank these people for their hos-
    pitality and come along.
RITA: Hello, Mary Margaret.

1938. MARY MARGARET *and* RITA *hoist a banner, donning the veils
    and cloaks of the Children of Mary.*

Do you reckon I look like someone off the pictures?
MARY MARGARET: We'll be late.
RITA: See? Deadset Ginger Rogers.
MARY MARGARET: Ginger Meggs is more like it.
RITA: And what does that make you, Little Orphan Annie? Eddie Grogan
    and Barry Carmody are hanging round outside the picture show last
    night…

EDDIE and BARRY *appear, sixteen.*

EDDIE: How you going, Reet?

BARRY: How you going, Reet?

EDDIE: Hey, Reet…

RITA: Eddie Grogan, grinning from ear to ear…

EDDIE: Anyone told you you've got legs like Ginger Rogers?

BARRY: Reckon.

RITA: Course, that wasn't all he said.

EDDIE: You flash your ginger, Rogers, and I'll give my Fred Astaire.

MARY MARGARET: What?

BARRY: You flash your ginger, Rogers, and he'll give his Fred a stare.

RITA: And he would, too.

MARY MARGARET: Would what?

RITA: Give his Fred a stare.

MARY MARGARET: Is that what they call it? Fred?

RITA: Fred I've never heard. Lots of others. Old fella. John Thomas. Wee Willie Winkie…

> *They are convulsed.* MOTHER JOHN *appears.*

MOTHER JOHN: We're waiting, girls.

MARY MARGARET: Sorry, Mother John.

MOTHER JOHN: You don't want us to be late at the shrine. Not today of all days.

> *She goes.*

RITA: Today of all days. Like Our Lady only has one feast day. One a week is more like it. The Immaculate Conception, the Purification, the Annunciation. It's a wonder there's not a feast day for her first period.

MARY MARGARET: I don't think Our Lady had her periods.

RITA: No. Her insides were stainless steel. She scrubbed them out once a year with Bon Ami.

MARY MARGARET: Stop it.

RITA: And baby Jesus was delivered in a cellophane bag.

> MARY MARGARET *hoists the banner. A hymn ahead of them.*

I'm too old for this lurk. This is my last procession.

> NEIL DONOVAN, *sixteen, appears, in school uniform, writing a letter.*

NEIL: [*as he writes*] 'I have been thinking about you a lot since I met you last Christmas.'

    He crumples the paper.

MARY MARGARET: Don't you want to make your debut?

RITA: I don't have to be a Child of Mary to make my debut.

MARY MARGARET: But if you want a certain partner…

RITA: Which certain partner would that be?

MARY MARGARET: Which certain partner. I'm not blind. Neil Donovan.

NEIL: [*as he writes*] 'Are you wondering why it's taken me this long to write?'

RITA: Is it that obvious? I don't know what to do. Thought I might write him a letter. But what can you say in a letter?

NEIL: [*as he writes*] 'Two months to the Leaving Certificate.' Shit. Brilliant.

MARY MARGARET: I'm sure he'd write back. He has nice manners.

RITA: And luscious lips.

MARY MARGARET: Yes, he does.

    NEIL *passes between them, close enough to kiss.* RITA *kisses* MARY MARGARET *on the lips.*

RITA: Luscious lips.

MARY MARGARET: There's more to life than lips.

RITA: I'll say.

    MARY MARGARET *is in her pinafore, with* MOTHER JOHN. *She is cleaning a brass vase.*

MOTHER JOHN: We believe you've been marked out for better things than shorthand and typing. Do you know what I might mean by that?

MARY MARGARET: No, Mother John.

MOTHER JOHN: I think you do, Mary Margaret. You're a good girl, all of us are sure of that. You have grace. Not just in the catechism sense. You have beautiful manners. And we want something good for you.

MARY MARGARET: I don't think…

MOTHER JOHN: What? What, dear?

MARY MARGARET: I don't think I have a vocation, Mother.

MOTHER JOHN: Everyone has a vocation. You don't believe you have a vocation to the religious life. Why not?

MARY MARGARET: Do I have to say?

MOTHER JOHN: I do want to know.

MARY MARGARET: I like boys. When I look at them.

MOTHER JOHN: Any boys in particular?

> MARY MARGARET *finishes the vase.*

I imagine they like looking at you. That is fine and healthy. I've never thought you were marked out to be a nun. You'll make a good partner to someone one day. That's the highest vocation of all, wife and mother. So we must train you for that.

MARY MARGARET: I don't... I don't see how you can be trained...

MOTHER JOHN: Mrs Donovan is looking for someone. She'd have a lot to teach you about the running of a household. She knows how to bring out the best in everybody. She likes you, Mary Margaret. I could almost say she's had her eye on you.

> NEIL *writes a letter.*

NEIL: [*as he writes*] 'They tell us: It's your last term, boys, use it well. But all I've been able to think about is you and you and you. And seeing you. We've started swot vac. I'm boning up on Ancient History and Physics. But what's the Law of Gravity up against the Rule of Rita? I'll get one of the kitchen staff to post this. The Housemaster would see the steam coming off the envelope. I've got...'

> RITA *reads it to* MARY MARGARET.

RITA: [*reading*] '... to get something off my chest.' Oh-oh.

NEIL: [*as he writes*] 'Last Christmas holidays I saw you, with one of the girls from the orphanage...'

MARY MARGARET: One of the girls from the orphanage...

RITA [*reading*] & NEIL [*as he writes, together*] : '... heading for the swimming hole at Horseshoe Bend. I followed you, thought I might jump in and bomb you. But when I got down there, I saw the two of you...'

> MARY MARGARET *gasps.*

It gets better. [*Reading*] '... taking your clothes off...'

NEIL: I suppose I should feel like a dirty old man.

RITA: [*reading*] 'But I don't. It was too beautiful.' Too beautiful, that's us.

MARY MARGARET: That's you. I'm one of the girls from the orphanage. He doesn't even know my name.

RITA: He knows where your appendix scar is. Too beautiful. I wonder if he played with himself.

MARY MARGARET: It did feel good.

RITA: Being perved on?

MARY MARGARET: Jumping in. I loved that.

RITA: You took a bit of persuading.

1962. The swimming pool. TIM *prepares to dive.* BROTHER CLEMENT *is below him with a whistle. Perhaps* NEIL *is watching.*

CLEMENT: Donovan. Arms up. Balance the weight. You've seen what to do. Do what the others do. Do it! Now!

TIM: [*coughing*] I can't.

CLEMENT: Come down off the board, Donovan. Turn around and climb down the ladder. Nobody else has climbed down the ladder today, Donovan. Nobody ever climbs down that ladder. It's a ladder that only goes up, Donovan. Except for you.

1938. The Donovan house. RITA *with* MRS DONOVAN.

RITA: It must take a lot of cleaning, Mrs Donovan.

MRS DONOVAN: We don't use this room much for everyday. For the girls' weddings, we slid back those doors and cleared the floor for dancing. Are you a dancer, Rita?

RITA: I'm no Ginger Rogers. But I don't make a fool of myself.

MRS DONOVAN: What do you know about me? No need to be timid.

RITA: You're married. He's Donovan and Cunningham. Three daughters, one son. You drive a black Humber. You take an interest in the orphanage. That's about it.

MRS DONOVAN: Do you want to know what I've heard about you? You're a girl with spirit. You're a handful. They said both about me. I have no secrets. My family were dirt-poor, nine children, no prospects. What I have now, this house, this garden, these lovely things, I'm deeply grateful for it all. I vowed I'd never pretend to be better than I was, a poor girl who married into all this. Would you like afternoon tea? I've made an apple cake.

She rings a bell.

Neil tells me he's asked you to his Valete. His dance. 'Valete' means 'farewell'. Were you surprised?

RITA: No.

MRS DONOVAN: That sounds confident. He might have asked a girl from the set down there. But we're pleased that he didn't. I wanted you to know that. [*Beat.*] What about your frock? I think we'll get something made. I know a good woman.

RITA: I was going to make something myself.

MRS DONOVAN: You can help choose the fabric. Now, the dance itself. Mr Donovan won't be free, but we'll drive down on our own.

RITA: I can get the train, thanks.

MRS DONOVAN: We can do the big shops. Perhaps we'll take in a show.

RITA: Hang on, who's robbing this coach?

MRS DONOVAN: I'm sure you'd like to apologise for that, and we'll forget it happened. [*Beat.*] Your mother's a good woman, Rita. She didn't bring you up to speak like that. An apology will clear the air.

> MARY MARGARET *brings in the tea tray.*

RITA: You're really working here? I thought that was a joke.

MRS DONOVAN: We don't call it working. Mary Margaret is coming to live in with us. Are we going to hear that apology? I do want us to be friends, Rita.

RITA: Why?

> *1962. The caravan.* SHANE *drags out a box. In it are mementos, a stack of letters. He finds one.*

SHANE: Shut your eyes. Now open them. Slow.

TIM: What is it?

SHANE: What does it look like? It's a stiffie.

TIM: What?

SHANE: A bloke's stiffie. He's drawn the outline of his thing.

TIM: His thing…

SHANE: His tool. His old fella. His cock. This thing.

> *He grabs* TIM*'s groin.* TIM *recoils.*

Standing up. The bloke traced it while it was standing up.

> *1938/1962.* BARRY CARMODY *appears, perhaps in either time frame.*

BARRY: You flash your ginger, Rogers…

TIM: Why?

SHANE: He was thinking about her.

TIM: About your mum? Is that what happens? It looks so big.

1962. A hotel. RITA *with a rack of glasses.*

BARRY: You flash your ginger, Rogers…

RITA: … and I'll give my Fred a stare, right.

BARRY: Me and Eddie Grogan. We were a couple of deadset lairs.

RITA: You were alright.

BARRY: Oh, those days…

RITA: … are dead, Barry.

She is going back to work.

BARRY: It's worked out well, Reet. Real well.

RITA: Thanks.

BARRY: Real well. Hasn't it, eh? Extra well.

RITA: Good, Barry.

BARRY: I'll tell you frankly. It was a leap in the dark. Anything could have happened to you. You could have let yourself go. But you look just as good as you ever did. Right off a Fantale box. A real movie star.

RITA: Rin Tin Tin…

BARRY: And you've fitted in real well. They like you. There's no two ways about it. You've hit just the right note.

RITA: Tell me what it is, I'll keep hitting it.

BARRY: I'm real glad you wrote that letter.

RITA: I'm glad you answered. You've been a lifesaver. Work's good. The boy's settling down. Soon as I pay a few bills we'll give you back your caravan and I'll rent us a little house.

BARRY: Good for you. There might be a promotion for you, somewhere down the track. Running the dining room, looking after the commercials. Hostess, kind of thing.

RITA: Where does that leave your mother?

BARRY: She's past it. I need someone with a bit more zip. And that's definitely you, Rita. I think we're a winning combo, you and me.

RITA: I better win myself back to the front bar.

BARRY: You're a real good sort. You know, if you hadn't gone and hooked up with Eddie Grogan…

1940. EDDIE *in army uniform.*

EDDIE: Hey, Reet. Suppose you're hooked up for tonight?

RITA: You suppose right.

> NEIL *passes. They circle one another in a fragment of a dance step.*

EDDIE: Not even one dance?

RITA: Not even one, Eddie.

EDDIE: Meet me after, then. Down the Horseshoe Bend. Send a gallant Digger off with a smile on his lips.

RITA: With a smack in the moosh. That's all I got for you.

> EDDIE *chuckles and goes.*

> *1939. The Donovan house.* NEIL *passes* MARY MARGARET. *He is in tennis whites and carries a racquet. She has a tray of used glasses.*

> BARRY *and* RITA *are still in the pub in 1962.*

BARRY: How did you get hooked up with him?

RITA: Ancient History, Barry. Not my subject.

> *She heads back to the bar.* BARRY *goes.*

MARY MARGARET: Did you win?

NEIL: We thrashed them. I made the match point. I think I must have pulled a muscle.

> *He unbuttons his shirt, kneading his shoulder. She is going.*

Do you think you could...?

MARY MARGARET: What?

NEIL: Work this for me?

MARY MARGARET: Oh. How do I...?

> *He takes off his shirt.*

NEIL: Take a grip here. Find the knot with your thumb...

> *She does.*

Ah.

MARY MARGARET: Sorry.

NEIL: No, it's good. You can go harder. Harder still.

MARY MARGARET: How's that?

> *He sighs, closing his eyes.*

Enough?

NEIL: Keep going. If you don't mind...

MARY MARGARET: Your skin feels… smoother than I thought it would be. Boys get so weathered, all that sun…

NEIL: You could do with a bit yourself. You're so pale. Lilywhite. The bits I've seen.

She giggles.

I meant your face and arms. What? I don't keep secrets from you.

MARY MARGARET: Well… you've seen more than my face and arms.

NEIL: Never! When?

MARY MARGARET: Two years ago. When Rita and I were on the riverbank, at the Horseshoe Bend.

NEIL: Was that you with Rita?

MARY MARGARET: Yes. It was me. Are you seeing her tonight?

He puts a finger to his lips.

She's made a new frock. Be sure and notice. Where are you going? Where are you seeing her?

MRS DONOVAN *is there.*

MRS DONOVAN: We'll need a mint sauce for the lamb. Are you in for dinner, dear?

NEIL: No. There's a bit of a dance on.

MRS DONOVAN: There's always a bit of a dance on. Your father likes to have some conversation at the table.

NEIL: Mary Marg's a good talker.

MRS DONOVAN: A man, I mean.

NEIL: He gets enough of me at the office, Ma.

He goes.

MARY MARGARET: He likes dancing, you know.

MRS DONOVAN: I know what he likes.

MARY MARGARET: I'll take these in…

MRS DONOVAN: I met Mr Donovan at a Bachelors and Spinsters Ball. I wore a borrowed frock, and a pair of old threadbare gloves, and had as much small talk as a doorpost. But Mr Donovan persevered. [*Taking the glasses*] I'll take these. You pick the mint. Mr Donovan likes your mint sauce.

She goes. MARY MARGARET *stays.*

1962. The yard. MARY MARGARET *sees* TIM *do a modest stunt on a bicycle.*

SHANE: Now no hands. It's underneath you. There you go.

TIM *disappears.*

I didn't mean go away! Timmy, come back!

TIM *reappears.*

TIM: Did you think I was going to leave town?

SHANE: We could join a circus. See? We'll do some fancy stuff.

TIM: Across the tennis court.

MARY MARGARET *runs off.*

Double dinka, doubla danka.

SHANE: Dinka danka.

TIM: Ganga. Gangaranga.

SHANE: Gangarangabanga.

TIM: Gangarangabangatanga.

MARY MARGARET *returns with a camera. She snaps them.*

MARY MARGARET: I'd like to be introduced, please.

TIM: This is Shane. From the caravan out the back of the pub.

MARY MARGARET: Oh, yes, I remember.

SHANE: You used to know my mum.

MARY MARGARET: We were at school together. I lived in the orphanage. Would you like afternoon tea?

TIM: No.

SHANE: You got any Coke?

MARY MARGARET: Coca-Cola? I'm afraid not. I could make chocolate milk.

SHANE *does a wheelie.* MARY MARGARET *snaps again.*

TIM: Stop that.

MARY MARGARET: Don't be mean, Timothy. I'll bring a tray out.

SHANE: Were you in the same class as Mum?

MARY MARGARET: I was, yes.

SHANE: You don't look old enough.

MARY MARGARET: That's a grown-up compliment. I'm sure my sons think I've always looked this old.

SHANE: How old are you?

MARY MARGARET: I'm a year older than my teeth.

SHANE: How old are your teeth?

MARY MARGARET: Too old to answer cheeky boys' questions.

> *She goes.*

TIM: She's thirty-nine. It says on her driver's licence. Born 1923. Let's go.

SHANE: I'm hungry.

TIM: Let's go.

> *1981. The bar.* TIM *with* SHANE. *They have drinks.*

SHANE: You didn't tell me what you do.

TIM: What I do?

SHANE: For a crust. What do you do?

TIM: What do you think?

SHANE: Lawyer.

> TIM *laughs.*

Something in an office. Something in a suit. I bet you look sharp in a suit.

TIM: Don't even own one. I work for the Opera Company.

SHANE: You a singer?

TIM: Note-basher. I play the piano. I'm what's called a répétiteur. Répétiteur… I had fantasies once. Of being a singer. Some kind of performer, anyway.

> *1962.* BROTHER CLEMENT *in the school hall. An out-of-tune piano accompanies.*

CLEMENT: Little Dutch boys on this side. Little Dutch girls on that side. Pair up. All the Jacobs line up here. All the Lenas here. I'm the windmill.

TIM: [*singing*] 'Little Mr Baggy Britches…'

> SHANE *and* TIM *dance.*

> > 'I love you.
> > If you'll be my Sunday fellow
> > I'll patch 'em mit purple, mit pink and mit yellow
> > And folks will say—'

CLEMENT: Lean in, girls. Boys, look a bit interested. She's your sweetheart.

> [*Singing*] 'Lena's been patching her Jacob
> Till he's got no britches at all.
> Ja, ja, Jacob…'

Kiss.

TIM: How do we do the kissing, Brother?

CLEMENT: 'How do we do the kissing, Brother?' Wouldn't you know it's Donovan? You act it, Donovan. You do it in the air.

The music continues.

SHANE: I'll kiss you on the lips.

TIM: In the air. Brother said.

SHANE: On the lips. You're my sweetheart. I'll trace my stiffie on a piece of paper.

TIM: Stop it.

SHANE: Well, I've got one now. See?

1981. The bar.

TIM: 'Little Mr Baggy Britches…'

SHANE: You got me.

TIM: You're not big on nostalgia.

SHANE: I'm big enough where it counts.

TIM: The heart?

They laugh.

SHANE: Let's get out of here.

TIM: Hang on. Alan's waving.

SHANE: Wave back. Come on.

TIM: He's calling me over.

SHANE: You got a nice place? Bet you have, bet you're well set up. You going to show me?

TIM: I'd better see what he wants.

SHANE: Tell you what I want…

He grabs the snow dome.

This. I'll hold onto this.

TIM: Why?

SHANE: Make sure you don't go without me.

TIM: I haven't said I'm going anywhere… John.

SHANE: I don't have to be John.

He watches TIM *go into the shadows.*

I can be whatever you want me to be. Whatever you want me to be…

1957. Outside Mrs Kennedy's house. EDDIE *has his knife. He flicks it open.*

EDDIE: It's a beautiful thing. A beautiful, terrible thing. And it's a part of me. Sometimes the best part of me, son. Sometimes the worst. But a beautiful thing. It can get a man into strife. Let alone a kid of… What are you now?

SHANE: Nearly seven.

EDDIE: Do a terrible lot of damage before he knows it. There's a law against this. And for a good reason. It's swift. Terribly swift. No going back once it's out. But beautiful. See?

SHANE *reaches for it.* EDDIE *closes it.*

You know what we're going to do? We're going to stash it away, out of harm's way. I told your mum I'd tossed it in the river but this'll be our secret, matey. Tell you what, you hide it. Where's a good spot, now?

SHANE: In the toy box on the back verandah.

EDDIE: Too easy to get at. How about under the house? You can slide in there easy. Go on. Good spot for it, under your grandma's house. That'd tickle her if she knew. But it's our little secret, matey. Yours and Dad's. Go on. No mucking round with it, but. Quick in, quick out. That's the Grogan motto.

RITA *emerges with luggage as* SHANE *runs off.*

RITA: Where's he off to?

EDDIE: Wanted to say goodbye to the chooks.

RITA: We should get going. While Mum's still at church.

EDDIE: Quick in, quick out.

RITA: Yeah. How much petrol you got?

EDDIE: We'll be right. Calm down, Reet.

RITA: I don't know about this, Eddie…

EDDIE: The boy needs a bloke around. So do you.

RITA: But how long will you stick?

EDDIE: Give you my word once. Ought to be enough.

RITA: And that bloody knife? What about that?

EDDIE: Six foot under.

> SHANE *comes back.* EDDIE *grabs the bags.*

Off we go, the three of us. Way it was always meant to be, eh? Eh, son?

> *They go.*

> *1942. The Kennedy house.* MARY MARGARET *and* MRS KENNEDY *are making up parcels for the troops.*

MARY MARGARET: I'm up to sixty words a minute.

MRS KENNEDY: You're a bright girl. I wish you'd been mine, instead of her.

MARY MARGARET: You don't mean that.

MRS KENNEDY: But I was given her for my sins.

> RITA *overhears this. She has a bag.*

RITA: You've got no sins, Ma. You've knocked off that much time in Purgatory you'll be first past the post on Judgment Day. They'll make you the patron saint of disappointed mothers.

MARY MARGARET: Have a lovely time.

MRS KENNEDY: That's all that matters, isn't it?

MARY MARGARET: She's doing what she has to do.

MRS KENNEDY: Here's this one sticking up for you. Why can't you take after her? She's learnt shorthand and typing. What have you ever done to improve yourself?

MARY MARGARET: Please, Mrs Kennedy—

MRS KENNEDY: And the minute you land a halfway decent job you throw it in.

RITA: If they won't give me time off that's their lookout.

MRS KENNEDY: And your loss.

RITA: There's plenty of jobs. Only one chance to see Neil.

MRS KENNEDY: Why isn't the boy coming home? Didn't occur to him his parents might like to see him?

RITA: No time. He's only got forty-eight hours. And he wants to spend it with me.

MRS KENNEDY: After you put the idea in his head.

RITA: He wrote and asked me. That must be the one letter you didn't steam open.

MRS KENNEDY: Please, Rita, don't do this. Please. Go in to work, apologise, get them to take you back. This is a fool's errand. The Donovan boy's never going to marry you.

RITA: You think it's marriage I'm after? Neil could be dead in six months.

MARY MARGARET: Rita…

RITA: Any of them could be. Barry Carmody might never get to wear them socks or eat that fruitcake.

MRS KENNEDY: Go on, then. Off you go. They say Brisbane's one big brothel these days. You'll be in your element.

Silence.

RITA: He does love me.

MARY MARGARET: He does, Mrs Kennedy.

MRS KENNEDY: I can see what he loves. And how long will that last?

RITA: How long will anything last? I'll settle for here and now.

She goes.

MARY MARGARET: You're too hard on her.

MRS KENNEDY: She's a fool to herself.

MARY MARGARET: Much too hard.

MRS KENNEDY: [*indicating the parcels*] Let's get these finished.

MARY MARGARET: She's been a good friend to me.

MRS KENNEDY: Not your only friend. You know there's nothing I wouldn't do for you, Mary Margaret. I've put the string down somewhere.

MARY MARGARET: My mother… Did you ever hear anything about her?

MRS KENNEDY: Those good Sisters have been mothers to you. That's enough.

MARY MARGARET: I'd just like to know… something. Even a name.

MRS KENNEDY *holds up heavy socks.*

MRS KENNEDY: What use would they have for these in the desert?

1962. Night. NEIL *and* MARY MARGARET *alone. She sorts photographs.* TIM *makes the Dutch plaits elsewhere, dancing slowly.*

NEIL: Colin was never involved in anything like this. Or Patrick. Why has he been singled out?

MARY MARGARET: I don't think it's a solo part, Neil.

NEIL: Very funny. You know they think he's a freak?

She shushes him sharply.

What if he is? He talks to himself. He can't make friends.

MARY MARGARET: He seems to have made one.

NEIL: He doesn't mix. He doesn't join in. He can't dive. He can't kick a ball. He can't stay vertical on a bike.

She points to a photograph.

Not alone. And sick half the year with chest complaints.

MARY MARGARET: Alright, we won't send him away to school next year. We'll pack him off to Wirth's circus.

NEIL: I've tried to understand him.

MARY MARGARET: To understand why he's not like Colin and Patrick.

NEIL: He doesn't have to act like Colin and Patrick. He doesn't have to act like anyone in particular. But I won't have him pooncing around the Town Hall stage in a dress.

TIM *wears the plaits, miming the moment of the kiss.*

MARY MARGARET: Then you tell him. I'm tired of cracking the whip.

TIM *is in front of his parents, holding the plaits.*

TIM: You want me to join in. I'm joining in this.

MARY MARGARET: Why don't you join in on something else?

TIM: I'm partners with Shane. If I drop out, who will he have to do it with?

MARY MARGARET: Perhaps there's no harm in it.

NEIL: Mary. You can go to your room, now. Tim, it's nearly bedtime.

TIM: It's not, not nearly. You don't even know what time bedtime is.

NEIL: Then go and read a book.

TIM: No.

NEIL: I beg your pardon?

TIM: I'm not giving this up.

NEIL: You'll do as you're told.

TIM: Uckpucka skittaswa. Grang grang grang.

NEIL: What?

MARY MARGARET: It's his private language.

NEIL: What language?

TIM: Uckpucka skittaswa. Grang grang grang.

NEIL: And what does that mean? What?

TIM: Uckpucka skittaswa. Grang grang grang.

NEIL: Tell me what it means!

TIM: Uckpucka skittaswa. Grang grang grang.

> NEIL *hits him across the face.* TIM *runs away.*

MARY MARGARET: I don't like hitting.

NEIL: He's got to be punished. There's an excursion coming up, isn't there? I wrote a cheque.

> MRS DONOVAN *comes to* TIM. *She has a copy of* Life *magazine.*

MRS DONOVAN: [*reading*] 'Ask not what your country can do for you, ask what you can do for your country.' See? A face full of purpose.

TIM: Go away, Gran.

MRS DONOVAN: He was speaking to all of us, not just his own people. He was given a great deal—a wealthy background, a fine education. And he's paid it all back, with dividends, running the most powerful country in the world. This man was born to lead. Your father admires him, he has Mr Kennedy's picture hanging in his office.

TIM: Between John the Twenty-third and Grandad.

MRS DONOVAN: You may not ever be in a position to do anything for your country. But your family… You'll be given wonderful opportunities, you know, more than other boys in this town.

TIM: They've stopped me going to the snow.

MRS DONOVAN: Every punishment has a reason, even if you can't see it. You're a very lucky boy. When you say your prayers tonight, you should thank God for what's ahead.

TIM: No Mister Baggy Britches and no Jindabyne.

MRS DONOVAN: No-one's life is easy, Timothy. Your father works very hard to give you the best. And look at your mother, where she came from…

TIM: A poor little orphan girl with no dollies or nice toys—

MRS DONOVAN: That's not funny, it's true.

TIM: And you found her on the doorstep in a shoebox…

MRS DONOVAN: You're turning into a very pert little boy. The nuns brought her up beautifully. She came to us at sixteen. You should be glad she did.

TIM: Why?

MRS DONOVAN: I was going to leave you this magazine with all these marvellous pictures, but I don't think you deserve it.

She goes.

1945. The railway station. RITA *gives a box to* MARY MARGARET.

RITA: I've had them under the floorboards. But Mum'd be bound to find them this time. There you go.

MARY MARGARET: It's heavy. I suppose it would be. Five years of love.

RITA: Five years of something.

MARY MARGARET: I feel wicked holding this.

RITA: You keep a good secret. You're a good pal. He says he always likes your letters. A ray of sunshine, he reckons.

MARY MARGARET: Does he?

RITA: Hey, I'll buy you a pressie this time.

MARY MARGARET: You don't have to.

RITA: I've never done a thing for you.

MARY MARGARET: You taught me the drawback.

A train whistle.

RITA: Hide that well, now. To think it'll be sitting under the Donovan roof, like a depth charge.

She runs off. MARY MARGARET *takes the box and goes.*

1962. Night. The caravan. In SHANE*'s nightmare,* EDDIE *stands over him with a belt.* RITA *finds him.*

It's okay. Shane, it's okay. Mum's here. Bad dream? We all have them. What was it?

SHANE: Can't remember.

RITA: Sure? Because if it was your dad—

EDDIE *gives* SHANE *a last lick of the belt and goes.*

SHANE: I can't remember.

RITA: I won't let any of that happen again. Never again.

SHANE: He'll be coming back, won't he? They'll let him out in the end.

Noise outside.

Who's that?

RITA: Dunno. Not him. Go to sleep. And don't worry about nothing.

BARRY *is outside, with a bottle of whisky.*

BARRY: You disappeared on me.

RITA: Your mother didn't give me much choice…

BARRY: She's still not convinced about you, Rita.

RITA: I work hard. I keep my trap shut. You tell me I'm popular. You were talking about a promotion a while back.

BARRY: And I talked to Mum. Then she went and had a word with your mother. You didn't tell me you were still married to Eddie.

RITA: We were never actually married.

BARRY: Or where he was. Where he is.

RITA: I told you I'd given him the flick. That's the truth.

BARRY: Not the whole truth. When's he getting out?

RITA: He's not coming here.

BARRY: He trailed you back here once before.

RITA: They've done a good job, those two old witches. [*Indicating the whisky*] And here's the golden handshake.

BARRY: Don't be bloody ridiculous.

RITA: If the old lady's got it in for me…

BARRY: The pub's only half hers.

RITA: I won't make trouble, I'll go.

BARRY: Where?

RITA: There's always a job somewhere. Lend me enough to get the car fixed and we'll be on our way.

BARRY: I wouldn't hear of it. Don't get upset, please, Reet. Come on, let's go inside.

RITA: Inside? The kid's asleep.

BARRY: The kid…

RITA: Slipped your mind, had it?

BARRY: No. He's a good scout. He won't mind stepping outside.

RITA: At this hour?

BARRY: Go on. Put him outside.

RITA: I couldn't do that.

BARRY: Won't hurt him. Just for a bit.

RITA: We can stay outside.

BARRY: Whose caravan is it?

RITA: Go easy, Barry, we'll have a nightcap out here.

BARRY: You going to keep me out of my own caravan?

RITA: Christ, you gave it to us.

BARRY: Gave you the use of it. We've got a lot to talk about, Rita. You've got a lot to tell me. I'd like to sit down in comfort.

RITA: I've got a pair of folding chairs. I'll bring them out.

BARRY: I want to look after you. Keep you here, keep you safe. The both of you. I think the world of you, Rita, you know that? Put the kid outside. Just for a bit.

The Donovan house. SHANE *is at Tim's window.*

SHANE: Timmy.

TIM *wakes.*

Can I come in?

TIM: Why?

SHANE: It's cold. Let me in.

TIM: What for?

SHANE: To stay, what do you reckon? I'll be gone before it gets light.

TIM: What happened?

SHANE: Nothing. Can I?

TIM: Course you can.

TIM *helps him in.* MARY MARGARET *comes out shining a torch.*

MARY MARGARET: What is going on? Is that Shane?

SHANE: I wanted to stay the night.

MRS DONOVAN: [*offstage*] What is it, Mary Margaret?

MARY MARGARET: Nothing. Just a stray cat. [*To* SHANE] You wanted to stay? Without asking?

SHANE: I asked him.

MARY MARGARET: Does your mother know you're here?

SHANE: No.

MARY MARGARET: Then go home this minute.

SHANE: I can't.

MARY MARGARET: Why not?

SHANE: Mum's having a party.

Silence.

TIM: Let him stay.

MRS DONOVAN: [*offstage*] Mary Margaret?

MARY MARGARET: If your mother wanted you to stay the night we'd have to make arrangements. And then you'd be very welcome.

SHANE *goes.*

TIM: A stray cat.

MARY MARGARET: Your grandmother gets nervous at night, specially when your father's away. Did you ask Shane in? That was very naughty.

TIM: Do you think I'm a stray cat?

MARY MARGARET: I think you're a very strange boy. Go back to bed.

TIM: Groonda deglar.

MARY MARGARET: Don't think I don't know what that means.

TIM: What?

MARY MARGARET: Something awful.

SHANE *throws tin cans at the caravan.*

BARRY: Cut that out!

He emerges, perhaps dressing.

I said cut it out, son.

SHANE: I'm not your son. Fuck off out of here.

RITA *emerges as* BARRY *grabs* SHANE *by the scruff of the neck.* SHANE *kicks him in the balls.*

RITA: Oh, crikey, Shane!

BARRY *pulls the belt out of his trousers.*

No, Barry.

She intervenes. He pushes her aside.

BARRY: Get out of it.

He grabs SHANE *and starts to flay him.*

Smart little bastard, aren't you?

1957. SHANE, *on his own, is beaten by* EDDIE, *who takes the belt from* BARRY.

SHANE: No! No, Dad!

EDDIE *goes.*

1945. A convent.

MARY MARGARET: Mother?

SHANE: Mum… Mum?

He picks himself up off the floor and goes.

MARY MARGARET: What was I called? When you took me? There must have been a note, or something.

MOTHER JOHN: You came to us by steps. Your mother had you in the Home, and left you there. Then, when you could walk and talk you were brought to us.

MARY MARGARET: But what was I called? Someone must remember.

MOTHER JOHN: Someone may remember. I don't.

MARY MARGARET: It must be written down somewhere.

MOTHER JOHN: Why should you have any other name? Nothing could be as lovely as Mary Margaret. Mary for the Mother of Our Lord, and Margaret is 'daisy', isn't it? I think we can do better than daisies. Madonna lilies, masses of them on the high altar. And something to set them off. Something blue. We'd love to help with the dress, too, but that's best left in Mrs Donovan's hands. Mrs Donovan… there'll be two of you now. But I'll still think of you as Mary Margaret. A beautiful name. Mary Margaret Donovan.

MARY MARGARET: Mary Margaret Donovan.

1962. SHANE *sits outside the caravan.* MARY MARGARET *brings a bundle of clothes.*

Is your mother here, Shane?

SHANE: She's at work.

MARY MARGARET: You're not at school?

SHANE: What does it look like?

MARY MARGARET: You may have thought I was pretty harsh last night. But Timothy's father was away, and I felt… responsible. Anyway, I was hoping to see your mother. I've brought some clothes. Tim's brothers have outgrown them, and I thought… I'll leave them. Perhaps I'll write a note. Explaining. You are cross with me. I'm sorry. I didn't mean to make you unwelcome. I want you two to be friends.

She stares at his legs.

What are those marks?

SHANE: Nothing.

MARY MARGARET: Show me.

SHANE: Rack off.

MARY MARGARET: Show me! Who did this? There was a party, you said.
    What sort of party?
SHANE: I never said nothing.
MARY MARGARET: Did she do this to you?
SHANE: No!
MARY MARGARET: She did, didn't she?
SHANE: No!
MARY MARGARET: Not your father?
SHANE: No. Another bloke.
MARY MARGARET: Who? Don't cry, please…
SHANE: I'm not. Rack off.

   She approaches. He withdraws.

MARY MARGARET: I won't hurt you. Don't be scared.
SHANE: You'll get her in strife.

*Vanessa Downing as Mary Margaret and Greg Stone as Shane Grogan
in the 1996 Adelaide Festival Centre/Playbox Theatre Company
production at The Space Theatre, Adelaide Festival Centre, Adelaide.
(Photo: David Wilson)*

MARY MARGARET: I won't. Poor Shane…

> *She loosens his clothes and looks at his upper back. She tries to comfort him. He yields, then pulls away.*

SHANE: Get out of it.

> *He runs away.*

> *Mrs Kennedy's house.*

MRS KENNEDY: Go carefully. She's cunning. She'll only bundle the boy off somewhere else. She can turn on sixpence, always could, turn on a threepence. The way she dropped Neil Donovan and took up with that deadhead Grogan, practically overnight. Though I suppose you're grateful she did.

MARY MARGARET: Shane's a good boy, isn't he? In spite of everything.

MRS KENNEDY: We'll have to wait and see. Time's been good to you, Mary Margaret. You're still a pretty thing, and those boys are credits to you.

MARY MARGARET: I hope we can salvage this boy.

MRS KENNEDY: Go carefully. I'll be praying.

> MARY MARGARET *with* NEIL *in his office. He stares at the photo of* SHANE *and* TIM *on the bike.*

NEIL: Two boys on a bike. You didn't say who he was.

MARY MARGARET: There was no point then. Now you need to know.

NEIL: Couldn't it have been some other kid?

MARY MARGARET: He has a look of her, doesn't he?

> NEIL *won't look at the picture.*

I've never known her to be cruel. Reckless, never cruel.

> *A* RECEPTIONIST*'s voice is heard on the intercom.*

RECEPTIONIST: [*voice-over*] Mr Donovan, I have the Bishop's House on the line.

NEIL: I'll ring back. [*To* MARY MARGARET] This is none of our business.

MARY MARGARET: It could happen again tonight, another party. I found an empty bottle of whisky in that caravan.

NEIL: Leave it alone.

MARY MARGARET: Don't you think we have some responsibility?

NEIL: [*indicating*] I'm up to here with responsibilities.

MARY MARGARET: Please, Neil. If we don't do something, we'll regret it for the rest of our lives.

NEIL: That sounds like something off a radio serial.

MARY MARGARET: I don't listen to the serials.

NEIL: Drop it, Mary. I won't tell you again,

MARY MARGARET: I won't be told. This is a matter of conscience.

She goes. He stares at the photograph.

1981. The bar.

ALAN: Do you know how long I've been doing semaphore over here?

TIM: Semaphore?

ALAN: Yes. Mauve alert. And you wouldn't come.

TIM: I was caught up.

ALAN: I'll say. La Wally says that guy is dangerous.

TIM: How would Wally know?

ALAN: Wal's never wrong. Not about trade. Don't go back. Stay here. There's safety in numbers, even old numbers like me.

TIM: I'm alright. I think I know him…

ALAN: No, you don't.

TIM: … and I have to be sure.

ALAN: You don't know him, lovey, and you don't want to know him! Wally's got the story. His friend Crystal dragged some number home from the Taxi Club. Called himself Jack. Got her coked off her face, rooted her senseless, then robbed her. At knifepoint.

TIM: Knifepoint…

ALAN: Took her pay packet, gold chains, everything. But left her with a nice deep cut across the chest, a warning to keep her mouth shut. Wal swears it's him. There's other stories round the traps. They all sound like the same guy. Jack the Stripper. Jack the Striper, actually. Scarred poor old Crystal from here to—

SHANE *is there.*

John. We were just going.

SHANE *holds up the snow dome.*

SHANE: Not without this.

ALAN: Tim? We have to go, don't we? To catch the late-night movie.

TIM: Do we?

ALAN: You don't want to miss it. *Looking for Mr Goodbar.*

TIM: That's not on tonight.

ALAN: I'm sure it is.

TIM: No.

SHANE: He says it's not on.

ALAN: Tim—

TIM: It's not on.

ALAN: It might be. Better be on the safe side. I think we ought to go.

TIM: Not yet.

ALAN: Tim, I was hiding behind screens before you were born.

TIM: Thanks, Al.

ALAN: Have it your own way.

> *He goes.*

SHANE: So what's happening?

> *They stay there.*

> *1962. The Donovan house.*

RITA: Just the way I remember it. Course, I was only here the once. The old girl's still with you?

MARY MARGARET: Not today. We're alone.

SHANE: I said what's happening, Timmy?

RITA: Cryptic little note you wrote.

MARY MARGARET: I thought it was better to meet here. We won't be interrupted.

TIM: What's happening, Timmy…?

RITA: Sounds ominous.

SHANE: Yeah. What's happening?

MARY MARGARET: Tell me… how much did you want Shane?

TIM: I hope you can tell me… John.

RITA: I wanted him a lot.

MARY MARGARET: And now, do you want him now?

SHANE: Tell me what you want. You want me?

RITA: How could I not want him? He's mine.

MARY MARGARET: Not just yours. Where's his father?

RITA: You wouldn't ask that if you didn't know the answer.

MARY MARGARET: I only think I know. Where?

TIM: What I want. That's a big question, this early in the night.

RITA: Where do you think? Satisfied?

SHANE: I think you can handle a big question.

MARY MARGARET: No. I know what that man did to him.

RITA: His father?

MARY MARGARET: That man, whoever he was, the other night. I saw the marks.

TIM: I want to talk. I want to listen.

RITA: I did what I could.

MARY MARGARET: Despite a skinful of whisky.

RITA: Jesus, did you bring the tracker dogs round?

SHANE: What do you want to hear?

MARY MARGARET: It wasn't just the beating. He was wandering the streets late at night. Shut out of his own home… if you can call it a home! So you could have a party.

RITA: What fucking business is it of yours?

TIM: I want to hear…

MARY MARGARET: I think children need chances. Not cruelty and neglect, opportunities. He's a good bright boy. He deserves the best.

TIM: I want to hear…

RITA: Look, why am I here?

TIM: Why are you here?

MARY MARGARET: Why are you here?

SHANE: Why am I here? You tell me.

END OF ACT ONE

ACT TWO

1981, the bar; and 1962, the Donovan house.

MARY MARGARET: I think you know the answer.

TIM: No. You tell me.

SHANE: Why do you reckon?

MARY MARGARET: I'll be direct. We want Shane to move in here.

RITA: That's direct, alright.

TIM: What if I made a body search? Right now…

MARY MARGARET: We'd like to look after him.

RITA: Just like that.

MARY MARGARET: I'm sure you can see the advantages.

SHANE: A body search…

MARY MARGARET: To Shane. To both of them. Two boys, the same age,
   facing the same challenges…

RITA: You want my kid.

MARY MARGARET: They could do a lot for each other.

RITA: So you want my kid.

MARY MARGARET: I want to see justice done.

SHANE: You mean a strip search?

RITA: Are you bent on taking everything off me? Everything that's ever
   meant something?

MARY MARGARET: How much does the boy mean to you, Rita? I saw him
   the next day outside that caravan. Alone and wretched.

RITA: Wretched? He's tougher than that.

SHANE: What do you want to find?

MARY MARGARET: If we reported you, Shane would be taken into care.
   You'd lose him anyway.

RITA: I'm not losing him, no way. I waited too long for him to let him go.
   He was my third. Did you ever lose one? Did you?

   MARY MARGARET *shakes her head.*

My first two I lost before I knew them, but Shane I carried to term.
Got him here safe and sound.

MARY MARGARET: Safe and sound…

SHANE: Well? What's the deal?

RITA: It was him and me all the way. Don't do this to me. It would kill me. I can't lose him.

MARY MARGARET: You don't deserve him.

TIM: What's the deal? Everything's a deal...

RITA: You won't take him. Out of my way. I said out of my way!

> *She goes.*

MARY MARGARET: Don't do anything stupid. Rita!

> *She follows* RITA *out.*

TIM: You want what I've got, don't you? Whatever that turns out to be? So I need to know what you've got.

SHANE: You'll see.

TIM: I mean, on you. What are you carrying?

> SHANE *produces a sachet of coke.*

I've never seen snow. The real stuff, that is.

SHANE: This is real, mate. Uncut. Two hundred bucks a gram. But for you...

TIM: Is that all you're carrying? John?

SHANE: I travel light. Look, I don't give a stuff, it's a deal, it's no deal. I'm gone.

TIM: No, Come home with me. Show me what else you've got.

SHANE: It might cost you...

TIM: Finish your drink.

> *1962. The caravan / the convent.* RITA *packs as* MARY MARGARET *pushes* MOTHER JOHN *in a wheelchair, perhaps circling her.* RITA *has the box of letters.*

MARY MARGARET: She used to bring me things, lovely things, a glass bead she'd found in the street, a peg doll got up as a little Dutch girl. This will kill her, she says. But I can't think about that. I have to consider only what's best for him.

MOTHER JOHN: You have three fine boys of your own. This one is no concern of yours. He's a ragamuffin. No better than a blackfella.

MARY MARGARET: He was beaten, Mother. There were welts all over his legs. She doesn't deserve him. And if she doesn't deserve him she shouldn't be allowed to keep him.

MOTHER JOHN: Rita Kennedy broke her mother's heart. This boy would break yours. I can't have that. You're our great success, Mary Margaret. We made sure Mrs Donovan noticed you, picked you out. You were worth the effort. You saved her son from bringing them shame. Saved him from his own shame.

> *Also 1945.* MARY MARGARET *opens the box of letters.* NEIL *is there, perhaps in uniform.* RITA *still packs.*

I must finish my beads. Today is the Joyful Mysteries.

> MARY MARGARET *takes out a letter and reads.* NEIL *is behind her. She reads out loud as he addresses* RITA. *Actors and director should decide who says what.*

MARY MARGARET [*reading*] & NEIL: [*to* RITA, *shared dialogue*] 'Keep your body a mystery.' Isn't that what Mother John used to tell you girls? It's no mystery to me. I've got it all mapped out. Every night I explore it. I'd make a good explorer, Rita. And I know where I'd plant the flag. I see you walking away from me, rolling those hips. I see those other blokes staring at you, tongues hanging out, ready for a good long drink. It's bloody hard, Rita. And the longer I'm away, the harder it is. See?

> MARY MARGARET *turns to a new page and stares at the drawing.* NEIL *goes, his eye on* RITA. MARY MARGARET *puts the letter away hastily.*

> *1962.* MARY MARGARET *goes with* MOTHER JOHN. BARRY *approaches the caravan.*

BARRY: Rita! Rita Kennedy!

RITA: Grogan, thanks. I know it's a courtesy title, but—

BARRY: Mum said you came in for your pay. Did you and her have another blue? You got a problem, you come to Barry. I thought we got that straight the other night. Packing?

> *She closes the bags. The box of letters still sits on the ground.*

Where the bloody hell are you going?

RITA: Away.

BARRY: Away. Away where?

RITA: I dunno. Just away.

BARRY: Why? Look me in the eye, Rita. Why?

RITA: They're trying to take Shane off me.

BARRY: What's he done?

RITA: You mean, what was done to him? Don't fret. No names, no pack drill. Anyway, I was the one that put him outside. I started this. And there's one way to finish it.

BARRY: Who's after you? Not the cops?

RITA: Might as well be. The Donovans. Mary Marg saw Shane on the loose that night. And she knows he got a hiding.

BARRY: A few licks of the belt. We've all copped worse.

RITA: She saw the marks.

BARRY: That makes it her word against yours.

RITA: She's got the law involved.

BARRY: The law. Them Donovans think they run the place. Don't let them bulldoze you. Stand your ground.

RITA: How? How can I? I feel cursed. Mother John taught us this poem once. 'The curse is come upon me, said the Lady.' We giggled, we knew all about the curse. Well, there's a real curse on me. Mum laid it on me, the day I went off with Eddy. 'Nothing will ever come right for you. You'll jonah yourself every step of the way.'

BARRY: Come up to the pub, we'll have a quiet drink…

RITA: I won't touch another drop as long as I live.

BARRY: Then I'll make you a good strong cup of tea, with three sugars in it. I notice things like that. Strong, sweet tea and we'll talk this over. You're in no state to make a decision.

RITA: I've made it.

BARRY: Don't be such a bloody mug. I've never seen you panic like this. Relax. You had a problem, you wrote to Barry. You got a bigger problem, Barry's still your man.

RITA: You reckon? What if Eddie Grogan lobs in the middle of all this? Where will I be then?

BARRY: I'll handle Grogan. And I'll handle the bloody Donovans. They're not the only ones with pull in this town. You're not going nowhere.

He picks up the suitcase.

RITA: Where are you taking that, then?

BARRY: I'm moving you and the boy inside. You're staying put.

He goes, leaving only the box of letters. She picks it up, studies it, then follows him.

SHANE *crawls under the Kennedy house.* MRS KENNEDY *feeds chooks. He finds his father's knife. He flicks it open.*

MRS KENNEDY: Who's that under there? Come on out. Quick. I'll put the hose on you.

SHANE pockets the knife and emerges.

Who are you?

SHANE: You know who I am.

Beat. She stares.

MRS KENNEDY: You look like you could do with a good scrub. What were you doing under there? Your toybox is still on the back verandah. I expect you're too old for toys now. Are you hungry?

SHANE: No.

MRS KENNEDY: You come inside and I'll feed you. But you'll have a good bath first. I'm not feeding a dirty savage.

She tries to take him in.

SHANE: Don't pull me.

MRS KENNEDY: What are those marks?

SHANE: Dirt. From under the house.

MRS KENNEDY: They're not dirt. They're welts.

He runs away.

Come back. Come back here. Shane?

1945. Mr Donovan's office. MARY MARGARET *and* MR DONOVAN.

MARY MARGARET: Wouldn't you want to know? If it was you, Mr Donovan?

MR DONOVAN: I don't think it should make the least difference to anyone.

MARY MARGARET: Tell me what you found. Or I'll go elsewhere. [*Beat.*] For God's sake! I was illegitimate. Men have been eating rats on the Burma railroad. I think I can take the news that some poor girl gave away a baby… [*Beat.*] What? Tell me. I'm sorry, Mr Donovan, I insist. I'm your client. Aren't I?

MR DONOVAN: Yes, my client.

MARY MARGARET: Then tell me…

MR DONOVAN: You were found with a deep head wound—not fresh—dried, suppurating. You were covered in bruises. You'd been thrown away. Not just abandoned—left to die. Your cry was so feeble it's a wonder you were found. You did insist on knowing.

MARY MARGARET: And now I know.

MR DONOVAN: You did insist. Thank God you found some kindness.

MARY MARGARET: Thank God.

MR DONOVAN: Nobody will ever hear about this from me.

MARY MARGARET: No.

MR DONOVAN: Not even Mrs Donovan.

MARY MARGARET: No.

MR DONOVAN: And I think you should keep this to yourself.

MARY MARGARET: I will.

MR DONOVAN: I'm very sorry, my dear.

MARY MARGARET: No. It gives me somewhere to come from.

1962. The river bank. TIM *and* SHANE.

TIM: That's the Southern Cross. It points down that way. This is what it must feel like, sleeping under the stars, the way they do in books. Wish we could sleep out here. Wish we could stay out all night.

SHANE: Then we will.

TIM: No. I've got to be home by eleven. They're out. I've got to beat them home.

He peers at his watch.

SHANE: You're always looking at your watch.

TIM: Sorry.

SHANE: Want some more Coke?

TIM: I wish I was more the way you want me to be.

SHANE: Have you ever left a penny overnight in a glass of Coke?

TIM: We don't have Coca-Cola… [in the house.]

SHANE: 'We don't have Coca-Cola in the house.' It comes out real clean. Shiny as new. What way?

TIM: What way what?

SHANE: What way do I want you to be?

TIM: Doesn't matter.

SHANE: Does if you said it. How do I want you to be that you're not?

TIM: I don't know.

SHANE: Yes, you do. Come on, how do I want you to be?

TIM: More like you.

SHANE: I'm like me. Why do I want two of me? You're not me. You're
    Timmy. There's nothing wrong with you.

TIM: Sorry.

SHANE: Except saying sorry.

TIM: And looking at my watch.

SHANE: Yeah. Chuck the watch.

> TIM *throws it in the water.*

Shit. I didn't mean chuck it. I meant do what you want. What do you
    want?

TIM: What do you mean?

SHANE: Here and now. What do you want?

TIM: What do I want?

SHANE: Apart from getting your watch back.

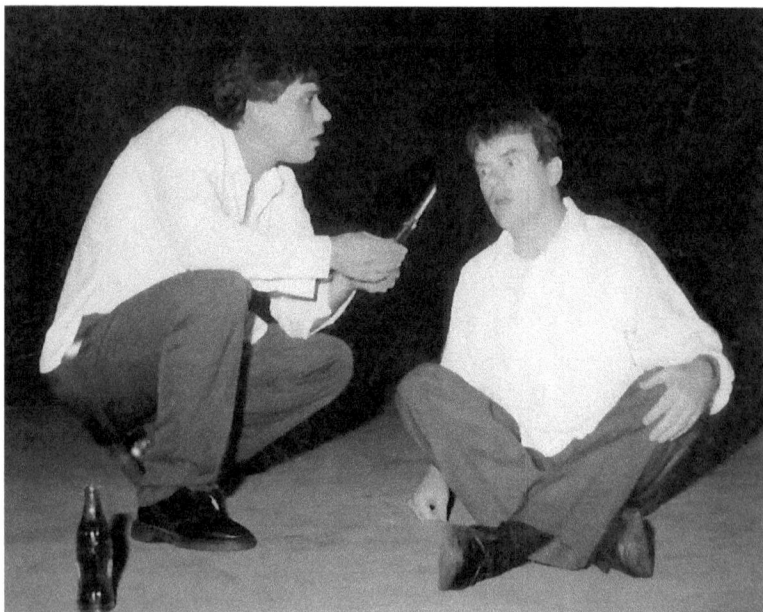

*Brad Weightman (left) as Shane and Michael Connor as Tim Donovan in
the 1998 Wollongong Workshop Theatre production, Wollongong, NSW.*

TIM: What do I want? I want… your biggest secret.

SHANE: My biggest secret. Easy. It's here. I've got it on me. [*Beat.*] See?

> *He reaches into his pocket and pulls out the flick knife.* TIM *reaches for it.*

Watch. Don't touch. It was my dad's. It could kill someone.

> *He flicks it open.*

TIM: Did he? Kill someone?

SHANE: Close enough.

> *He closes it.*

TIM: Give me a go.

SHANE: Too dangerous.

TIM: Please. I want to.

SHANE: Be really careful. Press it there.

> TIM *opens it. He slashes in the sky.*

TIM: The Southern Cross.

SHANE: That's enough. I'll close it.

TIM: I'll do it.

SHANE: Careful.

> TIM, *closing the knife, nicks the top of his thumb.*

TIM: I'm bleeding. Only a little bit.

SHANE: Give it here.

> *He takes it, holding it to his own thumb.*

TIM: What are you doing?

SHANE: Thumb to thumb. Quick.

> *They press thumbs.*

TIM: What does it mean?

SHANE: What does it look like? I'm for you and you're for me.

TIM: I'm for you and you're for me. I like that.

> SHANE *puts the knife away.*

What time do you think it is now?

SHANE: No time.

> *1945. The Kennedy house.* RITA *sews her Victory Dance dress, humming a ballad.* MRS KENNEDY *ushers in* MR DONOVAN.

MR DONOVAN: That's your frock for tonight? Very striking.

He glances at MRS KENNEDY, *who goes.*

I won't waste your time. I gather it's possible my son may have broached the idea of marriage with you.

Silence.

He was under great stress, living with death every day. Mrs Donovan and I don't believe he knew his own mind.

RITA: That's his business, isn't it?

MR DONOVAN: Not entirely. He's to be a partner in Donovan and Cunningham. Our trade isn't in groceries. We sell what we are. And that must be irreproachable.

RITA: I'm not with you.

MR DONOVAN: I think you are. My son needs to marry—

RITA: A silvertail?

MR DONOVAN: No. His mother was far from that, just a decent, good, religious girl…

RITA: And what are you looking at? The whore of Babylon?

MR DONOVAN: Let's keep this civilised. You've had a good war. Despite the Manpower regulations, you somehow gave up your job at the mills to work at the Railway Hotel.

RITA: So… you don't want him marrying a barmaid.

MR DONOVAN: Not one who's acquired a reputation for… openness, even carelessness. You've been in correspondence with other men.

RITA: Soldiers. They wrote to me, I wrote to them. I want to talk to Neil.

MR DONOVAN: We'd like to resolve this cleanly. If you'll give up any claim on my son, and hand over his letters, I have my cheque book here.

RITA: Cheque book? You can stick your bloody cheque book.

MR DONOVAN: You could name your own price, within reason.

RITA: Get out.

MR DONOVAN: All things considered, it's a very generous offer.

RITA: None of this means a damn thing. I want to hear from him.

MR DONOVAN: He's written you a note. I think you know his hand by now. It's the last communication you'll have from him.

He hands it to her.

I advise you not to fight. His mother and I didn't lose him to the enemy. We don't mean to lose him to you.

MR DONOVAN goes. RITA reads the note. She gathers up her discarded dress and goes.

1962. The Dovovan office. NEIL's suit is the same as his father's. The RECEPTIONIST's voice comes over the intercom.

RECEPTIONIST: [*voice-over*] Mr Donovan, a Mrs Grogan to see you. She has no appointment.

NEIL: Grogan…

RECEPTIONIST: [*voice-over*] She says you may know her as Kennedy.

NEIL: Send her in.

RITA comes in.

RITA: Hello, Neil. Looking good.

NEIL: Thank you.

RITA: Seventeen years. And you're not a day older.

The Donovan house. MARY MARGARET and TIM. TIM plays a wild improvisation on the piano.

MARY MARGARET: That can't be one of your practice pieces.

TIM: I made it up.

MARY MARGARET: It's very bold. It sounds like…

TIM: What?

MARY MARGARET: I don't know. Something fierce.

TIM plays on.

The office.

RITA: I've had the summons from Mary Marg. Tonight.

NEIL: Tonight?

RITA: She moves quick.

The RECEPTIONIST's voice on the intercom.

RECEPTIONIST: [*voice-over*] Mr Donovan, there's a Brother Clement on the line.

NEIL: Ask him to hold on.

RITA: You going to meet my eye? Or do I look too crook?

NEIL: You look tired.

RITA: I been doing a lot of running. But I'm not running no more. And I'm not giving up my kid, not over one mistake. So if you make me fight dirty—

NEIL: There'll be no fight. You can't win this.

RITA: You reckon?

The Donovan house.

MARY MARGARET: Tim… Timmy? Are you still friends with Shane?

TIM: Why?

MARY MARGARET: You haven't brought him back to the house. I wondered if you were still seeing him, still friends.

TIM: Why?

MARY MARGARET: Nothing. Just… Nothing. We like Shane.

The office. RITA *has an old letter.*

RITA: [*reading*] 'I look at her and it's your face I'm seeing. And not just your face. Why did I let you go? I let my life go then…'

The RECEPTIONIST*'s voice on the intercom.*

RECEPTIONIST: [*voice-over*] Mr Donovan—

NEIL: Hold the call! Give me that.

RITA: No, you listen. [*Reading*] 'I was a boy yesterday. Today I'm tied to all these people, a mother, a wife and two sons. My gut aches every day. Every night I sleep on a bed of knives…'

NEIL: Why are you doing this to me?

RITA: I just been wondering… was any of it true?

NEIL: I can't remember writing it.

She stares at him and holds up the letter.

I suppose some of it was true. At the moment I wrote it. Alright, it was true. It was all true.

RITA: But not the whole truth. Two sons, you said. There was a third on the way.

NEIL: How could you know that?

RITA: Arithmetic. The boys are the same age. This caught up with me just before I had mine. Any idea what it did to me, getting this?

NEIL: I was in a bad way myself… by the sound of it. I was writing under pressure.

RITA: I've heard that song before.

NEIL: It was a mistake, Rita. People make them all the time.

RITA: What was yours? Dumping me, or choosing her?

NEIL: That isn't what you came about. [*Beat.*] Can I have that back, please? Rita? [*Beat.*] None of it means anything now.

> *She looks at him and slowly shakes her head. She offers the letter… then snatches it back.*

RITA: No. But it might mean something to Mary Margaret.

NEIL: That'd be dirty, Rita.

> *She laughs.*

Alright. How much is it worth to you?

RITA: Out comes the fucken Donovan cheque book.

NEIL: Everything has a price.

RITA: Mine's my son.

> *She puts the letter in its envelope.*

You and her have got me backed against a wall. I've got to come out fighting.

> *The Donovan house.*

MARY MARGARET: Would you like to take Shane to the pictures tonight? [*Beat.*] I thought it would be nice for you both.

TIM: The pictures? On our own? Why?

MARY MARGARET: We're glad to see you make friends. Specially with a boy like Shane. We'd like you to see a lot more of each other.

> *The office.*

NEIL: You'll keep the boy. I promise you.

> *He reaches for the letter. She puts it away.*

RITA: Just to be on the safe side.

> *The* RECEPTIONIST*'s voice on the intercom.*

RECEPTIONIST: [*voice-over*] Mr Donovan? Brother Clement says he's due back in the classroom.

NEIL: Put him through. [*To* RITA] We'll settle this tonight.

> *She goes.*

> *1957.* MARY MARGARET *reads to* TIM.

MARY MARGARET: [*reading*] 'The mirror fell and broke into hundreds of millions of pieces. It was then that it really made trouble, much more than it ever had before. Some of its splinters were as tiny as grains of sand, and they were spread by winds all over the world. And in a small town one winter day, as the snow starts to fall…'

1962. SHANE *with* TIM *on the river bank.*

TIM: There's snowflakes flying through the air, but all mixed up with them are little splinters of glass, that look the same but they don't melt when they hit you. They get in under your skin, even in your eyes. Imagine, a piece of mirror going into your eye.

SHANE *shudders pleasurably.*

Something's going on at home. That's why they packed us off to the pictures.

SHANE: This is better than the pictures. Go on. He's out in the snow…

TIM: He gets a sliver of glass in his eye. Then he turns on all his mates. They run away. Suddenly there's a woman in white—

BROTHER CLEMENT *is there.*

CLEMENT: I saw you two heading down here. I know what you're up to.

SHANE: What are we up to?

CLEMENT: I've got no business with you, Grogan. I've got instructions for Donovan. Follow me.

TIM: Not now.

CLEMENT: From your father, Donovan. Follow me.

CLEMENT *goes.*

SHANE: Don't, Timmy.

TIM: I better. There is something up. They all had that look.

CLEMENT: [*offstage*] Donovan!

TIM: Brother must know something. He's got the same look.

SHANE: Stay here.

TIM: You stay. I'll come back.

He follows BROTHER CLEMENT.

The Donovan house. MARY MARGARET, NEIL *and* RITA.

MARY MARGARET: It would be a wonderful life for him. Fresh air, acres of bushland, water all around. He could take up rowing. He'll have great opportunities, excursions, career guidance, the best education. They're marvellous teachers, famous for it.

RITA: And what would I tell him?

MARY MARGARET: You want him to have a good life.

RITA: He'll have a good life. Staying where he is, with me.

The doorbell sounds.

MARY MARGARET: That will be your mother.

She goes.

RITA: Oh, Christ, now what?

NEIL: No. I gave you my word.

The classroom, exactly the same time.

CLEMENT: You've made trouble for me, boy. There's been a complaint from the Bishop's House. 'Mr Donovan is a pillar of the church, and you put his son into a skirt.' I had to ring up your father at his office, wait on the line till I could apologise. And when I've eaten my humble pie, your father says you're a creature from another planet. You speak your own language. 'Bring him down to earth, Brother. Make him one of us, Brother, that's your job.' So that's my job. Stand on that desk.

TIM: No.

He runs towards the door.

CLEMENT: No?

He drags TIM *up onto the desk.*

Stand. Up straight. No point looking towards the door. It's locked. Time for a private lesson. I've got boys brighter than you, Donovan. I've had dozens better than you, but you're the one that'll get put on the train in your straw boater. Don't think I'm against a privileged education. Leaders need that. Your brothers had the makings of leaders. You, Donovan, you're the makings of a rag doll. There's not a bit of sinew in you. Why are you smiling, Donovan?

TIM: Sinew in you. You made a rhyme.

CLEMENT: I made a rhyme. I'll give you a rhyme. A good one. Strop. And hop. I strop. You hop. This'll sharpen you up. Hop.

He catches TIM *across the legs.*

Higher. Hop. Don't drop. Hop.

TIM: I can't.

CLEMENT: It's hop or it's strop. There's no way down this time. No going down the ladder. You're out there.

SHANE *is outside the door.*

SHANE: Open up.

CLEMENT: We'll ignore that. Hop. Don't drop. Hop.

He swings. TIM *calls towards the door.*

TIM: Uckpucka!

CLEMENT: What?

SHANE: Uckpucka!

SHANE*'s trying to break down the door.*

CLEMENT: Tell him to go away, Donovan. Any damage he does I'll take out on your hide.

TIM: Uckpucka skittaswa. Grang grang grang.

CLEMENT: That language. Your father told me all about that.

He swings.

Now you translate.

TIM: Uckpucka.

CLEMENT: Translate. What does it mean?

The sound of breaking glass.

The Donovan house.

MRS KENNEDY: I saw the marks. I'll stand up in court. If your own mother speaks against you, they'll listen. I'll tell them you dumped him on me once. Three months she left him.

RITA: While I got my life fixed up! I'm not a dumper. I came back for him soon as I could.

MRS KENNEDY: You and that Eddie Grogan, making a fresh start, turning over a new leaf. You're a fool to yourself, Rita, and you always were. Look around. The boy's being offered a prize, a good family that can afford to give him the world. You're not going to stand in his light.

RITA: You're not getting hold of him, none of you.

MRS KENNEDY: I'll go to the police and lay charges.

RITA: But will they stick? Neil?

MARY MARGARET: Neil?

NEIL: Rita's allowed something very wrong to happen. But we have her word that it won't happen again. You said it yourself, Mary, he's a good, strong, healthy boy. Most boys his age are covered in bruises and bumps. The courts see cases of real brutality all the time. This matter would look pretty feeble. I think we'll put the whole business aside.

He glances at RITA. MARY MARGARET *sees.*

Now, if you'll excuse me, I'm in court myself tomorrow…

He goes.

MARY MARGARET: Neil? Neil!

She follows.

MRS KENNEDY: Just like always. Go on, jonah yourself, every step of the way.

RITA: You bloody old witch. It's you that wants to jonah me.

MRS KENNEDY: What in the name of God can you do for him?

RITA: I can pick him up from the pictures.

She goes.

The classroom. More breaking glass. BROTHER CLEMENT *is swinging at* TIM.

CLEMENT: That's two panes, Grogan. Every breakage is coming out of Donovan's hide.

TIM: Uckpucka.

CLEMENT: A private language? Nothing's private here. Translate.

BROTHER CLEMENT *connects.* TIM *screams, loud.*

SHANE: Uckpucka skittaswa. Grang grang grang.

SHANE *kicks through a panel of the door.*

CLEMENT: Right, Grogan…

He drags him in.

You've just sealed your doom, son. Wanton vandalism. You'll pay for that door, and the broken windowpanes.

SHANE: You were bullshitting. You said you had a message from his dad.

CLEMENT: The message is The Strop. Now I'll have the same for you too, father or no father.

TIM: Uckpucka skittaswa grang…

CLEMENT: What are you saying?!

SHANE: Fuck you. He's saying fuck you, you bastard.

> *He grabs for the strap.* BROTHER CLEMENT *throws him to the floor. He cuts his head open.*

Glass…

CLEMENT: You put it there. Look, knee deep.

SHANE: Blood.

CLEMENT: It's your fault. Let's stop this nonsense. Now, Grogan! Get out, the both of you.

> SHANE *pulls out the knife.*

What is that? Give it here…

> *He grabs for the knife.* SHANE *bares the blade and stabs* BROTHER CLEMENT, *who gasps and falls to the ground.* TIM *gets down off the desk.* BROTHER CLEMENT *whimpers.* TIM *stands over him, then starts to kick him hard in the guts.* BROTHER CLEMENT *groans.*

> *1981. The bar.* SHANE *puts on his jacket.*

SHANE: If we're going, let's go. Cold night out. Better be warm at your joint.

TIM: Is it the same knife?

SHANE: The same knife as what?

TIM: Where do you keep it? In your jacket? Or is it like the movies, down the side of one boot?

SHANE: Whatever you're on, mate, I want some.

TIM: What does it feel like when you stick it in? Same as the first time?

SHANE: You reckon I'm carrying a knife? But you asked me back home.

TIM: To see what happens.

SHANE: What if you got hurt?

TIM: Anyone can get sliced. Slashed. Skewered. But I'm not just anyone, am I? Not just someone who wants you. I'm someone who knows you. Will that make it harder?

SHANE: I'm gone.

TIM: Not without me.

SHANE: Giving orders now?

TIM: I'm talking blood to blood.

SHANE: You're talking bullshit.

TIM: I'm not. First night in ages I'm not. You've got a blade. I cut myself on it once. Blood brothers, we said. Brothers till death, weren't we? Maybe you've seen a lot of death since then. I have. I see death every day. People stick it to one another every hour on the hour, screaming away at the top of their lungs, pretending they're dying for love. And I bang away underneath them, pretending to be an orchestra. And every night I come in here and talk about movies, the same fakery, the same fucking fakery. Shane wasn't fake. He was the real thing. One night on a riverbank. Once and forever. And now I'm a répétiteur. I repeat and repeat and repeat and repeat. The same tunes, the same lines. See, most people never have to face the fact that at the right time, the right place—

SHANE: Shut the fuck up.

TIM: —they're capable of anything. Who said that?

SHANE: What do you want from me?

TIM: I want to look something in the face, even if it's the last thing I see.

SHANE: You want to neck yourself, mate?

TIM: Don't bullshit me now, because that tells me you're scared. Shane was never scared. Was he? Come home. Now. Let's see what happens.

A long silence.

SHANE: Okay.

TIM: Before we go—

SHANE: Fuck…

TIM: This is simple. Say who you are.

SHANE: You know anyone can answer that question?

TIM: Your name.

SHANE: I told you. John.

TIM: Your name.

SHANE: John!

TIM: Your real name.

SHANE: John! John is who I am.

TIM: Jack? Jack the Stripper? Jack the Striper?

SHANE: John.

TIM: Say your name. Just once. Shane. Then we can go.

SHANE: This bloke you want me to be, what did he do for you?

TIM: Come home and I'll tell you.

SHANE: What did you do for him?

TIM: I made him use his knife.

SHANE: You reckon?

TIM: I fucked his life up.

SHANE: Nobody does that.

TIM: You reckon?

SHANE: You're in charge.

TIM: Oh, please…

SHANE: If you're not in charge, you're dead. One or the other.

TIM: I'm not either.

SHANE: I thought you looked real smart, mate, real sharp, but you're a big disappointment. You're just one more dribble-shit queen that wishes he was dead.

TIM: No! I want to know—

SHANE: Why I'm here, yeah—

TIM: No! Why I'm here.

1945. MARY MARGARET *holds Rita's box of letters.*

MARY MARGARET: Because she has a hold on him. Like a spell. You'll see. The things he writes to her… he's not himself.

MRS DONOVAN: Should I show Mr Donovan?

MARY MARGARET: I think you should. But quickly. I will have to return them. She wanted them kept secret. I've broken a promise. But I don't feel she's right for him.

She offers the box. MRS DONOVAN *takes it.*

The Victory Dance at the Town Hall. MR DONOVAN *on the bandstand.*

MR DONOVAN: We all know why we're here. You can see our thanks and our prayers in our faces, and in the way the hall's been dressed by the ladies' committee. Today we gathered at Sacred Heart to mourn the men who didn't come home. Tonight we're here to thank and cheer the men who did. It's the end of conflict and fear and waiting, the beginning of peace, the start of a new age. And by the look of the spread in the supper room I'd say the ration books might just as well have gone right out the window, but no names, no pack drill. On behalf of the diocesan committee, it's my great pleasure to welcome you to this Victory Dance. Now I'll hand you over to Mr Music himself, Cyril Staines and his Melody Makers.

Jaunty dance music. RITA *passes.* NEIL *watches.*

EDDIE: Hey, Reet! Rita Kennedy! Long time no see.

NEIL: I'm sorry.

RITA: Four lines by special delivery. No drawings. Shortest note you ever wrote.

She turns away from him.

EDDIE: And still the hottest thing on two legs.

RITA: Who is, Eddie? You or me?

EDDIE: Quick too. Quick as a flash. Hey, remember? Flash your ginger, Rogers…

RITA: Yeah. And I just might. I bet Fred's ready for a stare.

EDDIE: A good long one, Reet.

They start dancing. NEIL *watches. They go.*

MR DONOVAN: This is a new world. Tonight's a night for beginnings.

MRS DONOVAN *and* MARY MARGARET *appear. They don't see the men.*

MRS DONOVAN: Don't be anxious. The dust will settle.

MARY MARGARET: He won't come.

MRS DONOVAN: He knows he must. Everyone's gone to so much trouble.

MR DONOVAN: She'll do well by you. She'll make a good partner, and in the end that's what counts.

MR DONOVAN *passes* NEIL *to* MARY MARGARET. *A romantic ballad.* MRS DONOVAN *dances with* MR DONOVAN.

MARY MARGARET: I love this tune.

She starts to hum it.

NEIL: I've done a disgusting thing. And here I am, dancing. I can't.

MARY MARGARET: You must. People want to see you. They're so glad you're here, and in one piece. I'm glad, Neil.

NEIL: I've done something terrible.

MARY MARGARET: Look me in the eye! You're a wonderful man, a brave man. I used to watch you coming into Mass behind your sisters. They were so pale. You were dark, as though you spent all your time in the sun. And so handsome.

They dance. MARY MARGARET *steers* NEIL.

Everyone's looking at you.

NEIL: I'm a piece of shit.

MARY MARGARET: You're home. Everybody wants you to be happy. We'll all do whatever we can. I want you to be happy, Neil. I'll do whatever I have to do.

She sings along with the band.

NEIL: I never knew you had a voice.

1957. A churchyard with the crèche figures of Joseph and Mary. MRS DONOVAN *brings on the baby.*

MRS DONOVAN: The Donovan set, that's what the nuns call these. Your grandfather bought them for the parish. The whole set—the shepherds, the little baby lambs. And the wise men who come at...?

TIM: Epiphany.

MRS DONOVAN: Epiphany, very good. And up there is the light to guide them here. The brightest star that ever was.

TIM: Not brighter than the Southern Cross.

MRS DONOVAN: Oh, yes.

TIM: Not brighter than Sputnik.

MRS DONOVAN: Much brighter than Sputnik, much much brighter. The Star of Bethlehem. Shining down on this Holy Family. I hope you remember your grandfather in your prayers.

She goes. TIM *looks up at the star.*

1962. MARY MARGARET *kneels alone among the Nativity figures.* RITA *approaches.*

RITA: Poor old Baby Jesus. There's a crack in the back of his head.

MARY MARGARET: That's in the moulding of the plaster. Every baby has a crack there.

RITA: Mine had to have seven stitches in his forehead. He'll be scarred up here for life, could have lost an eye. [*Beat.*] This was always Ma Donovan's job.

MARY MARGARET: She can't manage the kneeling anymore.

RITA: So you're earning a bit of extra grace. Where are the shepherds?

MARY MARGARET: We save those for Christmas Eve. Something for the children to watch out for. I'm very sorry.

RITA: About the shepherds? I'm sure they'll make it.

MARY MARGARET: About Shane.

RITA: And I suppose the wise men will clock in eventually. Take this back. Don't insult me.

She holds an envelope stuffed with money.

MARY MARGARET: I heard you were going away. I thought you might need it.

RITA: Barry Carmody's selling up. We'll start somewhere fresh, somewhere in the warm. Have a proper home for Shane when he gets out.

MARY MARGARET: Please take it.

RITA: I wouldn't take a thing from you. The one moment the Donovans could have done something useful, when a twelve-year-old boy went on trial—

MARY MARGARET: For killing, Rita. He killed someone.

RITA: The one time he really needed help you turned your backs…

MARY MARGARET: He stabbed a man. Not just any man, a religious Brother. He kicked him when he was down.

Helen Morse (left) as Rita Kennedy and Janet Andrewartha as Mary Margaret in the 1995 Playbox Theatre Company production at the CUB Malthouse, Southbank, Melbourne. (Photo: Jeff Busby)

RITA: After all those grand plans, education and friends and a place on the rowing team.

MARY MARGARET: How could we know he'd turn out to be dangerous?

RITA: That Brother was dangerous. And no-one ever said that in court. But the fear on your boy's face…

MARY MARGARET: After what he'd seen, are you surprised?

RITA: What if Shane was there to rescue him?

MARY MARGARET: That was never said.

RITA: What if he was? They didn't put your kid on trial.

MARY MARGARET: So it's Timothy's fault?

RITA: I don't say that…

MARY MARGARET: You'd like it to be anybody's fault but yours. Nothing's ever your fault. You're a big bleeding heart. And the world keeps doing the dirty on you. You're never responsible, for yourself or anyone. It wasn't you that teamed up with a gaolbird, wasn't you that let a twelve-year-old boy carry a knife.

RITA: I never knew he had the thing!

MARY MARGARET: There's a lot you missed. Like the marks on his body. It was me that found them, me that did something about them. That's love. I tried to do something for him, I tried to give him a chance in life.

RITA: You tried to buy him, because he's the only one that's ever spoken your boy's language. The only one that's ever loved him. [*Beat.*] You wanted to hit me, didn't you? Lucky you didn't. The frame of mind I'm in, I'd knock your block off. Don't worry, Mary Marg, you'd go straight to Heaven, wouldn't you? All those good works…

MARY MARGARET: What would you know about Tim?

RITA: The day Shane brought him home, you came after him like a copper. And all that was in his eyes was fear. But he wasn't born in love, was he?

MARY MARGARET: I don't see how you'd know.

RITA: Let's just say I know.

MARY MARGARET: And Shane was? With a father like Grogan? He was born in the gutter. Born with no chance. And that's your fault.

RITA: I don't have to listen to this.

MARY MARGARET: You do! Rita, what happened to you? We took all our clothes off once, one summer night. All those years of bathing in a calico chemise, and suddenly there you were and there I was. Skin on skin. You told me I was lovely, but you, you were the loveliest thing I'd ever seen. You were a goddess.

RITA: Oh, spare me…

MARY MARGARET: You were. You had it all.

RITA: I'm off. [*Offering the money*] Take this. I'll throw it away…

MARY MARGARET: Why did you let it all go?

RITA: Let it go? That's rich.

MARY MARGARET: All those other men.

RITA: What other men?!

MARY MARGARET: Don't pretend. All through the war, I saw things…

RITA: You saw a bit of kiss and cuddle and a few wandering hands. Nothing ever went beyond the hotel verandah.

MARY MARGARET: I happen to know that's not true.

RITA: How can you happen to know anything? Come on, I'm dust behind the door. What do you know?

MARY MARGARET: You gave me that box of letters…

RITA: Yeah. You gave them back. Oh. But you read them first.

MARY MARGARET: He knew what you were doing. You told him everything.

RITA: You nong. You bloody great nong. How long have you lived with him? And you haven't worked him out yet? I gave him what he wanted. He'd ask the juicy questions. I'd send the juicy answers. And you swallowed it all, all the bullshit. I suppose you told the world?

MARY MARGARET: Oh, God.

RITA: Not the world. Just the old couple. His world.

MARY MARGARET: God forgive me.

RITA: God's done well by you, good girl like you. Gave you what you wanted. But he's a cunning bastard. He makes the bed. And you have to lie in it.

She is going. MARY MARGARET *stops her.*

MARY MARGARET: I'm not loved. Is that the worst thing you can say to me? [*Beat.*] Look at me. I'm not loved. You think I haven't always known that? I used to wake up in the maid's room under the roof. I'd know the moment he came home. I'd hear every sound—door opening, shoes coming off, Neil creeping up the stairs, trying not to stumble, not drunk, just reeling from you. I'd hear him stumbling about underneath, I'd hear the springs of his bed as he settled, and I'd lie there and hold myself, touch myself, seeing myself burning in the pits of Hell, but touching myself, wondering, what happened? What did he do to you? With you, on you, in you, how did all the juices run together, where did you do it, how many times, what sounds did you make? I knew there had to be sounds, because even on my own I couldn't stop the sounds, and they had to be bigger with two. And you two... you two together... I could imagine...

She sinks among the crèche figures. After a moment, RITA *moves to comfort her. Finally* MARY MARGARET *subsides.*

RITA: Oh, Christ. Look at me. Look at the both of us. Back where we were.

RITA pushes her aside, and goes, putting the money down and leaving MARY MARGARET *alone among the figures.*

1938. MARY MARGARET *is alone on the riverbank, naked.* RITA *is perhaps already in the water.*

MARY MARGARET: What if someone's watching?

RITA: Let them.

MARY MARGARET: I feel weird.

RITA: You look lovely. So pale and shivery. Beautiful skin.

MARY MARGARET: Is it?

RITA: Milky white. I can see your appendix scar.

MARY MARGARET covers it.

If there is someone watching that's not the first thing I'd cover. But suit yourself.

MARY MARGARET stays there.

1962. Night. SHANE *and* TIM *also on the riverbank.*

TIM: What time do you think it is now?

SHANE: No time.

TIM: Now it's your turn. You get what you want.

SHANE: What I want. I want... I want us in there.

He points to the river.

TIM: Now? It's so dark.

SHANE: Yeah.

TIM: Could be dangerous.

SHANE: Yeah. Come on. We'll swim to the other side.

RITA: How long are you going to stay there?

MARY MARGARET: They can see us from the bridge.

RITA: There's nobody on the bridge.

> SHANE *has stripped and dived into the water. Like* RITA *he is perhaps only a voice now.*

TIM: It's too cold.

SHANE: It's warmer in here. Dive.

RITA & SHANE: [*together*] Look at you. You're shivering.

MARY MARGARET & TIM: [*together*] I'm cold.

SHANE: The longer you stay out there…

RITA: … the colder you'll be.

MARY MARGARET: Here I come.

> *She is gone.*

SHANE: Come on, this'll warm you up.

TIM: I'm coming. Where are you? I can't see you.

> *1981. The bar.*

SHANE: Shane, come back!

> ALAN *returns.*

ALAN: 'Shane, come back.' What is this, *Kindergarten of the Air*? That was poor little Brandon de Wilde watching Alan Ladd ride off into the sunset. Shane, come back. And they tell you queens hate westerns. Seven-four. I'll be kind. 'Hello, Bedford Falls, Merry Christmas.' Tim? Tim! Timotheena!

> TIM *runs into the street.*

TIM: Shane!

> *1957.* MRS DONOVAN *crosses* TIM*'s path. She gives him the little snow dome.*

MRS DONOVAN: Happy birthday, Timothy.

TIM: Why is there snow? We don't have snow at Christmas.

MRS DONOVAN: It shows us how it was that first Christmas. Shake it. Then you'll see how it truly was, all those years ago.

> MRS DONOVAN *goes.*

1981. TIM *runs to catch* SHANE.

TIM: Shane! I want an answer…

> SHANE *grabs* TIM, *putting a knife to his throat.* TIM *drops the snow dome.*

SHANE: Here's your answer, cunt. 'Why am I here? Why am I here?' Where I was, it was fucken cold. The cold come up through the floor. No-one told me why. I worked it out for myself. It's cold because it's cold. And you, you dribbling piece of shit, you got to wait for someone to tell you. Here's why.

> *He might be about to cut* TIM.

No. You want it too much. But you can't have it. Your whole fucken life, show me this, tell me why, hold me up, cut me loose, turn me on. And tonight take me home, let me in, just 'cause you think you know who I am—

TIM: I do!

SHANE: You don't fucken know me. You don't know shit about me. You stopped knowing me the last time you saw this. And now you want it again. Do it your fucken self.

> *He throws* TIM *down beside the snow dome.*

Cut yourself open on that.

TIM: I don't want to die. I just want to know I'm alive.

SHANE: You're shivering.

TIM: I'm cold.

SHANE: Then get on home.

TIM: I wanted to say I'm sorry. That's all…

SHANE: That's nothing.

> TIM *starts to go.*

I wrote you a letter once.

TIM: I never got it. What did it say?

SHANE: You'll never know.

> *He is gone.*

> MARY MARGARET, *aged six, passes with the peg doll.*

TIM: What's that?

MARY MARGARET: She's a present. She's Dutch.

TIM: Is it your birthday?

MARY MARGARET: I don't have a birthday.

TIM: Everyone has a birthday. How old are you?

MARY MARGARET: Six.

TIM: Then you must have birthdays.

MARY MARGARET: How old are you?

TIM: I'm twice your age. I'm twelve.

She sees the snow dome.

MARY MARGARET: What's that?

He holds the doll while she takes the snow dome.

SHANE *comes on.*

SHANE: I'll kiss you on the lips.

TIM: In the air. Brother said.

SHANE: On the lips. You're my sweetheart. Maybe I'll trace my stiffie on a piece of paper.

RITA appears with Neil's letter.

RITA: [*reading*] 'The longer I'm away, the harder it is. See?'

She finds the drawing. She laughs.

MARY MARGARET: Why is there snow?

TIM: It's Christmas. Mary and Joseph and the baby in the manger.

She shakes it.

See?

All four are among the Nativity figures. Snow starts to fall. It delights them.

Just the way it was.

MARY MARGARET *runs happily through the falling snow.*

THE END

www.currency.com.au

Visit Currency Press' website now to:

- Buy your books online
- Browse through our full list of titles, from plays to screenplays, books on theatre, film and music, and more
- Choose a play for your school or amateur performance group by cast size and gender
- Obtain information about performance rights
- Find out about theatre productions and other performing arts news across Australia
- For students, read our study guides
- For teachers, access syllabus and other relevant information
- Sign up for our email newsletter

The performing arts publisher

www.ingramcontent.com/pod-product-compliance
Lightning Source LLC
Chambersburg PA
CBHW050021090426
42734CB00021B/3360